Publisher:

Star's Edge International®
237 North Westmonte Drive
Altamonte Springs, Florida 32714

ISBN: 0-9626874-8-0

W0009392

Table of Contents

Section I The Path to Enlightened Master

Section II Building Momentum

Foreword

In terms of income and expansion, we were very
fortunate in 1987 that the Avatar technology was
embraced by so many of the leaders of the human
potential movement. These pioneers already had
skills in marketing courses and seminars. We
trained and licensed them to deliver Avatar. It
was the product that they had been looking for.
Overall, we were happy to see them prosper.

However, in terms of creating a cooperative
alignment toward creating an enlightened
civilization, we were not so fortunate. Many of
these same pioneers turned out to be excessively
competitive, lone ranger types whose business
acumen was much more evolved than their sense
of social responsibility.

Seeing Avatar commercialized into another
me-empowerment technique, at the sacrifice of
awakening a social consciousness, did not make
us happy.

So in 1991, we made changes in our advertising
appeal, our training emphasis, and our licensing
standards. Typical of the inexperienced, we made
too many changes. The pendulum swung to the
opposite extreme.

We attracted the savants of awakening social
consciousness: writers promoting peace,
metaphysicians integrating the great mysteries,
backpack environmentalists, and volunteer social
workers. These were all wonderful people, kind-
hearted, aligned, each with exceptional social
values, but their ability to conduct successful

business was worse than awful. They went broke, and the expansion of Avatar began to slow.

So again, somewhere in 1993, we made adjustments—but smaller adjustments.

First, we began to coax the Masters who were commercially successful to pay more attention to the social role of Avatar. The goal was not to change their profit motivations, but to broaden and expand their motivations. And we began to coax the Masters who were socially conscious to learn a little more about business.

We listened to many viewpoints, made many introductions, and were delighted to see that a balance could be struck between running a successful Avatar practice and continuing to live in a spiritual way that contributes to the creation of an enlightened planetary civilization. What a beautiful alignment! These beings achieved enlightened Master.

The *Avatar Master's Handbook* is about that balance. It is a How-To book aimed at Masters who want to begin (or continue) the practice of delivering Avatar.

It is also a reference for Avatars who are considering becoming Masters. Many will find the information in Section I of the handbook a welcome clarification on many things, including the use of primaries.

Section I

The Path To Enlightened Master

All the difficulties in the world today are merely secondaries to
an enlightened planetary civilization. —H

Chapter 1
Inspiration

(From a talk by Harry Palmer at the Grand Hotel in Gardone Riviera, Italy, on April 19, 1997.)

Something is reasonable as long as it fits with the way you structure your consciousness. This is very important. This is the most important thing I am going to say tonight. *Something is reasonable as long as it fits with the way you structure your consciousness.*

This is a principle that is explored in depth on the Wizard Course.

Consciousness is structured by the assumptions you make, by the beliefs you accept without question, and by the decisions you make.

The same idea may seem reasonable to one person, or it may seem unreasonable to another person. It depends on how it fits into the structure of the consciousness that views it. You could call this structure of assumptions, beliefs, and decisions a mind.

Some people look at an idea and say, "Oh, that's very reasonable." Why? Because it fits into the structure of consciousness they think with.

Other people look at the same idea and say, "That's completely crazy." Why? Because it does not fit into the structure of consciousness that they think with.

But it is the same idea.

Inspiring is awakening a viewpoint that realizes that something that seemed impossible can actually be done.—H

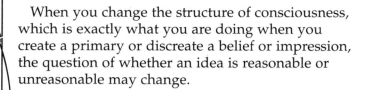

When you change the structure of consciousness, which is exactly what you are doing when you create a primary or discreate a belief or impression, the question of whether an idea is reasonable or unreasonable may change.

Trainers see this all the time. Someone comes to do the Master Course and within the structure of consciousness they come with, it seems unreasonable to them that they will ever deliver Avatar. Or maybe it seems unreasonable to them that they will ever do the Wizard Course. Or maybe it seems unreasonable to them that they are participating in the creation of an enlightened planetary civilization. Then they do the Master Course, and suddenly these ideas do not seem quite so unreasonable.

Someone does Avatar with you, and they start the course with some limitation that to them is entirely reasonable. "Oh, I can't do that. I can't make myself happy." And what happens? After the course, the same limitation that they had when they began now seems entirely unreasonable. Have you seen this? There has been a change of mind.

Maybe you are asking yourself, "Is there something that I consider beyond my ability that in fact is reasonably within my ability?" Well is there? What you think of as an impossible dream might be reasonable if you thought differently.

Let's look at this idea of creating an enlightened planetary civilization.

Did you know that some of the cathedrals in this country took over eight centuries to build? Eight-hundred years!

Some creations take a long time. They take even longer if you count the years that people dreamed about building a cathedral but still thought it was an impossible idea. How many years did they spend going, "Well, someday..."

Some creations take longer than they need to because people become discouraged at how long they are taking and give up on them. "Eight-hundred years to finish this cathedral? Oh, forget it."

That kind of discouragement can infect a whole generation. No one sets any bricks for years. The idea of the cathedral that had begun as a reasonable possibility is now considered an impossible dream. Consciousness has been changed by the currents of life.

But encouragement is also infectious. The Italian Renaissance was a period of infectious encouragement.

One day someone comes along, and the idea of completing the cathedral is raised again. Maybe the person who comes along is a dreamer or a visionary. Maybe they are following a hidden agenda to sell something else to the workers. Anyway, they have some gift of persuasion, and the work begins again. What is a twenty-year delay in a project that takes eight centuries?

So the idea is embraced by a few others, and the work begins again. Slowly at first. Maybe these people are dreamers or visionaries, or maybe they have hidden agendas. But the work begins. Maybe it's only a little work. Maybe just a few bricks are moved, and a plan is agreed upon. Maybe the only commitment is to gather on Sundays and pass some time working together. Share a picnic and enjoy the sun.

But with every stone that is placed, with every bucket of mortar, the possibility of actually creating a cathedral starts to become more real. People believe in it. This belief restructures consciousness. A crazy idea becomes a reasonable project again.

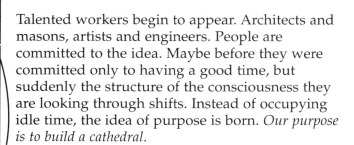

Talented workers begin to appear. Architects and masons, artists and engineers. People are committed to the idea. Maybe before they were committed only to having a good time, but suddenly the structure of the consciousness they are looking through shifts. Instead of occupying idle time, the idea of purpose is born. *Our purpose is to build a cathedral.*

As the cathedral begins to take shape, there are fewer doubters. There is less room for doubt. One day it even becomes unreasonable to doubt. Doubting becomes an indication of selfish misalignment.

Maybe it is discovered that one of the doubters stole some bricks or a beam from the cathedral and used it to build his own house. Maybe the theft isn't discovered until after the doubter is dead and gone. When it is discovered by a future generation—someone finds the altar stone of the cathedral over the doubter's fireplace—the doubter's memory is tarnished forever. Forever! There is no possibility of redemption. The doubter's reputation is ruined. They were doubting for their own selfish ends, and now everyone knows it.

This is horrible, but it does happen. Time reveals the truth. Maybe you don't think it is important how you are remembered by others. But **you** remember. It is a secret that separates you from the unity of life. A secret that separates you from your own enlightenment.

There are a few people who steal Avatar and use it for their own selfish ends—maybe to make a few bucks or to get someone to go to bed with them. If you talk to them, they will say, "You can't create an enlightened planetary civilization. It's not possible." Their dishonesty makes them doubters.

They hope it is not possible, because they have been stealing the bricks that were supposed to build the altar. Do you know what I am talking about?

They may not be found out in their lifetime, but eventually one of their students will come to you and understand that the purpose of Avatar is to build an enlightened planetary civilization. In that moment they will see that the person who sold them an altered version of Avatar was really nothing more than a selfish thief.

And the person who stole Avatar, the one whose dishonesty wouldn't allow them to align with the rest of us to create an enlightened planetary civilization, is exposed. Yes, it has happened. The person's reputation is tarnished forever. Forever. That is so much worse than having to review the Master Course or do a walk for atonement that there is no comparison. This is not a good vibration, so I won't talk about it anymore.

I'll tell you a story. There are three stonecutters, and they are all cutting stones. The first stonecutter is asked, "What are you doing?"

He answers angrily, "I'm cutting stones as any idiot can see."

He is angry, because every day is the same. He gets up and cuts stones. His life has no purpose that he can see, and he is unhappy.

The second stonecutter is asked, "What are you doing?" He is irritable. "I am cutting stones so I can raise a family and afford a nice house." He will die an unhappy, selfish man in a nice house. He has served only himself.

The third stonecutter is asked, "And what are you doing?"

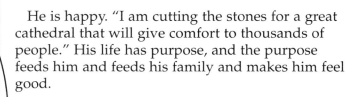

He is happy. "I am cutting the stones for a great cathedral that will give comfort to thousands of people." His life has purpose, and the purpose feeds him and feeds his family and makes him feel good.

The Goal of Life

An enlightened civilization is an idea that life has been working toward since the first creature appeared on this planet.

If you fired an arrow, stopped it in its flight, and sighted along the arrow, you would see where it was going. If you stop life in flight and sight along it, you will see that it is headed toward an enlightened planetary civilization. It is like building a great cathedral, only it will comfort everyone.

In 1987 chance favored a prepared mind, and the route to enlightenment was developed into a path that all could travel easily. Previous routes to enlightenment were traveled with great suffering and sacrifice. By comparison, Avatar is easy.

There were many elements that had to be addressed before the real purpose of the technology of Avatar would be seen as creating an enlightened planetary civilization. There were many decisions to be made. A way had to be found to keep the workers fed. Skills had to be learned.

Companions and helpers had to be found. Some contributed for a few weeks or months and grew discouraged at the size of the job, but a few stayed. A few noticed that just living to collect stuff was not really satisfying. They needed a purpose.

Pretty soon there were Avatars, there were Masters, and there were Wizards. And there were Star's Edge Trainers.

Creating an enlightened planetary civilization is no longer an impossible dream.

Eventually every individual must decide where he or she stands in relation to this idea of an enlightened planetary civilization. Is it reasonable to you? Tonight, new Masters, it is your time to decide.

How Do You Define Success?

If your goal is to be a multimillionaire living behind security fences, driving overpriced automobiles and spending hours with brokers, accountants, and lawyers, think twice about becoming a full-time Avatar Master. This is not an "Earn $10,000 a month in your spare time" deal. Only a few Masters ever earn that kind of money.

But, if you are not motivated to collect a lot of stuff or generate a lot of envy in people you don't really like, and you do enjoy living simply, meeting interesting people, and learning more about life, then by all means commit to being an Avatar Master.

A commitment should be the result of a rational process rather than an emotional process. Emotional commitments, whether driven by fear or desire, are very risky to your future integrity and honor.

The real profit from delivering Avatar goes beyond money. You leave behind you smarter, happier people. You become a smarter, happier person. Whatever your struggle or suffering, you know there is a payoff. You are working to protect an entire planetary civilization against future outbreaks of man's most deadly disease— ignorance.

Commitment

Contributing to the creation of an enlightened planetary civilization can take many forms. It does not necessarily mean that you quit your job and become a self-employed Avatar Master. That is only one option. Maybe you can do the most good by continuing what you are doing and using your influence to steer people toward greater care and tolerance. Maybe you can follow your profitable profession and deliver to an occasional student in your spare time or at a co-delivery with other Masters. Maybe you can partially or completely convert services you already deliver to Avatar courses. Maybe you can scale back working for others and transition into marketing and delivering Avatar with partners. Maybe you can affect legislation, media, or public opinion toward a more favorable environment for the planetary expansion of Avatar. Maybe you can add a little adventure to your retirement or spend your vacation doing something more productive than nursing a sunburn.

What are your options? They are discovered by using a combination of personal experiences, imagination, and reason. Rate your options by the same criteria you rated your goals in the beginning of the Master Course.

Exploring options is usually a 24- to 48-hour process. The advice to sleep on a proposal before you make a commitment is good advice. But finally, pick a direction or a plan of action and commit to it. Your commitment has power. It's a stable point in a chaotic world. It's a foundation for inspiring friendships. It is the power of your commitment that will determine your success or failure in any endeavor.

Here is a story that motivational speakers like to tell. Three frogs are sitting on a lily pad, and two decide to jump off. How many frogs are left on the lily pad? Someone in the audience always calls out, "One."

"No," the speaker says, "there are still three. Two of them decided, but they didn't commit any effort to acting!"

Commitment is backing up your primary with action. Undertake something.

Even if you are on the right track, you'll get run over if you just sit there.
—Will Rogers

Chapter 2
Growing Beyond the Terrain

In native state, awareness is singular, undefined source.

Creations, Agreements, and Changes

There are three apparent, interwoven universes that awareness functions in: 1) the universe of self, 2) the universe of the other, and 3) the shared physical universe. Creations, agreements, and changes, respectively, are the principle elements of these universes.

The problem is that the method of operation (creating, agreeing, or changing) that is successful in one universe may not succeed in another universe. For example, creating with **certainty** is very successful in the universe of self, but the same certainty may look like arrogance from the viewpoint of the other or an uncompromising stubbornness in relation to the physical universe.

1. Universe of Self (I am)

Awareness manifests itself in the universe of self as a mental recognition of *I am*.

The universe of self is composed of intentions, viewpoints, beliefs, emotions, and thoughts. Successful operation in this universe is achieved by acquiring the ability to manage these mental creations. (The sum of *I am's* mental creations is called **mind**.)

The tool for managing the mind is the Creation Handling Procedure (CHP). The mind is never resisted, dominated, nor created over. These three efforts—resistance, domination, and creation over (pretense)—are what trap awareness into intentions, viewpoints, beliefs, emotions, and thoughts.

With the Avatar materials, successful operation in this universe is accomplished by assuming an *I am* awareness that is separate from the mental processes. In the basic materials, thought, emotion, and belief are brought under control. In the more advanced materials, viewpoints and intentions are brought under control. And the Wizard materials address beingness itself, which is the gateway to and from the universe of self.

Within this universe, when *I am* makes a primary, the primary manifests as a self-enveloping experience. If there are any secondaries, they can be re-owned, experienced, and discreated.

2. Universe of the Other

Awareness manifests itself in the universe of the other *as perceived by* or as *I am*.

as perceived by *a remote viewpoint that imagines*

The universe of the other is composed of unknowns, projected motivations, identities, and assumptions. A basic assumption is that the universe of the other bears a resemblance to the universe of self.

Successful operation with the universe of the other is achieved by assuming control over your own assumptions, identities and projected motivations, and then offering a predictable, defined presence, while respecting the undefined presence of the other.

Rapport, common concerns, and patient

communication pave the route to reaching agreements. Compassion makes for equitable agreements. Integrity is an alignment of the agreements with a purpose beyond selfish concerns.

The sane purpose behind these agreements is to regulate a mutually satisfying exchange. The exchange may be goods, services, information, beliefs, affection, companionship, respect, admiration, security, or anything that either party finds valuable.

Broken agreements trap awareness in the universes of others.

3. The Physical Universe

The physical universe is a reality that *I am* recognizes as space, substance, tendency, motion, and time. *I am's* mind colors this reality with various interpretations and importances.

Substance is a mixture of matter and energy. Tendency is a higher order of intention (divine intention or nature) that compels substance into organized patterns of motion (biological evolution and physical laws). Time is the duration of a change.

Successful operation of a self in the physical universe is dependent upon establishing an objective viewpoint (perspective) that can observe, predict, and align its effort with tendency. Reasoned results are achieved by using mind and effort to steer substance and motion into imagined forms or circumstances.

When this is done spontaneously, without reasoning, it is called instinct or intuition.

Awareness manifests as the *space* of the physical

universe, and, as already discussed, harmonics within this space as *I am* or *as perceived by*. (The heart of unmanifest awareness can be reached by successively discreating all *as perceived by* definitions, all *I am* creations, and finally, all space. It's quite an enlightening trip.)

Confusion of Universes

The major reason people have trouble living successfully (i.e., achieving their goals, creating relationships, or being happy) comes down to a confusion of universes. They mistake the universe of the other for the universe of self and *I am* awareness is replaced by an *as perceived by* awareness. Or they employ a method they learned in the physical universe to the universe of the other to force a selfish agreement. Or they employ a tool (CHP) that works in their private universe to try to operate in opposition to the **tendency** of the physical universe, e.g., trying to discreate gravity or aging.

People who are ungrounded (i.e., responding inappropriately to their surroundings) have simply confused universes. Often they fashion the universe of self after the physical universe and then struggle with cause-and-effect relationships. What cause will make me happy effect?

The truth? Causes are physical universe phenomena. They move things or hold things still. They are localized events of the overall tendency of the physical universe. They make things grow or decay, but they don't produce happiness.

Happiness is an intentional creation of the self universe: *I am happy.* Of course the self can believe in all sorts of appropriate reasons for being happy or unhappy, but the bottom line is that the self decided.

Sometimes a person resists something in themselves and projects it into the universe of the other. It becomes the unspoken thing that they are always trying to come to agreement with the other about (actually it should be handled as their own creation with the CHP). So the attempt to reach agreements unravels and a relationship breaks up. Why? A confusion of universes. They are not really interacting with the other. They are living in the mind. The interactions are really monologues.

There is also the person who employs a style of operating that was successful in the physical universe (hard fact, cause-and-effect systems, limits and freedoms) to their self universe. The result is a being who is always figuring on self. What caused me to think this, why that, why me? No source. No spontaneous creative freedom. All of their primaries are preceded by secondaries. (Their primaries, you see, are really reactions.) They feel that all the events of their life are predetermined by past events and that there is nothing they can do about it, except maybe explain them. They believe they are either lucky or unlucky. They feel powerless, victims of circumstance.

It's amazing when you realize that the inventively cruel bully engaging in international or domestic violence and the unconditionally loving astrologer who can't keep a job are both suffering from the same impairment: they believe themselves to be victims of circumstance.

If someone is confusing universes, you can sometimes sort them out with one of the following: have them find differences between 1) two objects, or 2) between a present time observation and a similar memory, or 3) between someone they are having a conflict with and someone similar they once knew. This is only a quick patch. The real solution is doing Avatar to the full expected results.

Universes and the New Avatar Student

Think of these universes as three concentric spheres. In the middle is the private universe of self. In a healthy state, this universe has the least definition. It is flowing and flexible, pliant and supple. The next sphere is the universe of the other. In a healthy state, this universe contains agreed upon customs, rules of conduct and manners, but it is still flexible to cooperative adjustments. The outside sphere is the physical universe. In a healthy state, it is solidly defined and governed by cause-and-effect relations. In short, it is predictable. Physical events have determinable causes. Miracles in this universe are rare.

Your potential Avatars often begin in a condition just the opposite of the above. Their private universe of self will be very solidly defined: an inflexible asserted ego. The universe of the other is hidden under resisted identity projections. The physical universe appears as a chaotic flux governed by unpredictable chance.

As a Master, you are faced with one of the toughest tasks that anyone can undertake. You are going to coax your student into operating deliberately in their private universe of self. This is quite a trick since you have to operate through and beyond your own assumptions.

It's a big jump for a person to wake up from the *as perceived by* to the *I am* of his or her own private universe.

That's the first essential awakening on the path of Avatar.

Delivering Avatar to the Wrong Universe

Sometimes Avatar Masters pull the student back into the universe of others (interactions) to fulfill some interaction need. This can have the effect of strengthening the student's social skills and puffing up egos all around. The result is that the student learns to operate more successfully in the universe of others. This is certainly a gain, but in actuality the course has been delivered to the wrong universe. The Avatar Master has missed the essential goal of awakening self-realization in the other.

Later the student may turn to the Master for help saying something like, "I'm still feeling sort of depressed."

"Feeling depressed" is a universe-of-self phenomenon. The student never mastered operating in the self universe. Do you see? What's even worse, the inept Avatar Master may now sit down for a heart-to-heart talk, sharing wisdom and pulling the student back into operating in another universe. That is bad therapy. It doesn't last.

An Avatar Master who doesn't bring a student to self-realization can expect the student to become codependent on certain agreements with the Master. This is identity modeling. It is why disciples cling to cult gurus.

Truth and Universes

Truth has a different quality in each universe. In the universe of self, truth is faith in what one believes. In the universe of others, truth is agreement on what is to be mutually believed. In the physical universe, truth is what is, i.e., the products of tendency, physical reality, natural laws.

Faith achieves truth when there are no secondaries to the belief that one expresses to oneself. Truth in the universe of self can be changed by self (and no other).

Agreements achieve truth when there is complete trust and no betrayals. An agreement is the offspring of two or more minds. It has a life of its own, a developmental path that leads to a manifestation as physical universe substance. Once made, it cannot be turned off or discreated by a single viewpoint. (Reference and compare: multidimensional viewpoint in the Wizard materials.)

Because the agreement, once created, exists independently of the minds that made it, it can only be changed by a new agreement by the same minds.

Breaking an agreement drops you into the pretense of victim, locked in a struggle with an unyielding secondary, which is really only the abandoned agreement.

Natural law, physical sciences, are factual truths about the operation of space, substance, tendency, motion, and time. At the human level of distinguishing, they are independent of faith or agreement. Gravity does not care if you believe in it or not; you still fall. It does not care if minds agree to it; it is what is regardless of agreement.

So speaking the truth depends upon which universe a being is speaking about. I am _____, we are _____, it is _____ can all express something quite different and still be true.

Awakening in the Universe of Self

Despite the illusion, the universe of self is not intrinsically a cause-and-effect universe. There is only one self, and the only thing that can create an effect on it is itself. Interaction in the self-universe is either the result of prior creations, broken agreements, or deceptions by disincarnate entities (Reference: the Wizard Materials).

Face it. No one can make you feel or think in a way you don't prefer unless you let them. Granted there are tricks of persuasion and deception and pain-induced reactions, but these are short-term experiences. Only your resistance allows them to influence you long-term.

The desire to be right (or make another wrong) may have you resisting experiences months or even years after the actual event. It is not unusual to find a student being mentally influenced by people who are long dead and gone. So admitting to your own mistakes and forgiving others is very good medicine. Confession and forgiveness: the quintessential religion. *

Add gratitude and sacrifice to complete the essential structure of religion.

Test it. Put a complete stranger in a corner and see if there is anything he can say that will elevate your mood or make you angry. Unless you're in real bad shape, nada! A stranger is in the corner talking. Period. He doesn't influence you, because you are not deceived nor have you assigned source to him. You haven't given him permission to influence your private universe.

There is an ancient Egyptian initiation in which a disciple is led into a room full of people who shout criticisms. They hurl insults and invalidation. They make fun of the way the disciple looks. And just when the disciple is on the verge of tears, the master whispers in the disciple's ear, "Observe, these are criticizers. Their role in life is to criticize. That's what they do. Don't take it personally."

The universe of self is a source universe. The path to success and happiness in this universe is the recovery of source. (By the way, this is not, as the dictatorial ego may proclaim, the path to success and happiness in others' universes or the physical universe.)

Why Avatar Exists

Self-realization is about taking control of who you allow to influence your private universe. The truth is...well, you know.

This is a bigger dose of responsibility than most people can easily swallow. In most cases it is an overdose. It is not recommended that you approach someone who is suffering psychic scars and declare that they are solely responsible for how they engineer their private universe. This is not useful knowledge to them and will make you very unpopular. The psychic scars are real. The deception is about who created them, who keeps them created and why. Let them sort it out themselves with the Avatar tools.

Live deliberately is an urging not to let the physical universe or others (including the disincarnate entity phenomena that are discussed in the Wizard materials) dictate the design of your private universe. Wake up!

Self-Realization

Self-realization is knowing that you are, **and operating as**, the sovereign lord and creator of your universe. Knowing this as truth, but not knowing how or choosing not **to operate as**, is the source of the self-degradation that complexifies so many religions.

Avatar is not solely a spiritual message. It is the tools for learning **to operate as** a spirit.

Many talk the responsibility talk, but only a few walk the responsibility walk. Thanks to the efforts of Avatar Masters and the tools of Avatar, thousands are now making daily progress on their responsibility walk.

Chapter 3

The Power of Primaries

Primaries are wonderful things. In the universe of self, they create mental states or remove self-limitations. They change how sensations are evaluated (perception) or how one defines and identifies oneself.

When they are made from a near definitionless state of source, they can also influence the universe of the other and the physical universe.

In the universe of the other, a primary creates an intentional pressure or urging to act in a certain way. The primary can be verbally communicated, as in the case of a direct order, or it can be telepathically communicated, as in the case of a magic spell or an entity handle. The power of the person making the primary and the receptivity of the person receiving the primary determine if the primary will manifest. (Intuition may be the effect of a universal tendency on your universe.)

Some people, particularly Avatar graduates, have attested to changing their physical condition and even the structure of their bodies with primaries. It does happen. Others have altered or even reversed a sequence of cause-and-effect events. Tales of miracles abound.

Even when no miracle is created, a primary has the effect of refocusing your attention on a path of opportunity leading to the manifestation that you are intending. The primary acts like a road map. A route to your destination is marked.

A primary is the appearance of a creation. A secondary is the reappearance of a creation.

Secondaries

Existing conditions (default patterns) can be reactivated by a primary. These are called secondaries.

In the physical universe, the default patterns are the physical laws of science. It's extremely difficult (though maybe not impossible) to discreate physical laws like gravity or entropy.

Alignment with deeper and deeper source awareness can overcome even the most stubborn secondary (though often the primary disappears as well).

In the universe of self, the power that reactivates the secondary is never any greater than the power that is making the primary. It's you! So persistence (*and now the primary*) will eventually create the self-universe reality that you prefer.

Statements that reflect your relationship with the world are true if you decide they are true. Statements about conditions and events in the world are true if they reflect the agreement of the participants.

Reality Implies Limits

Most of you can stand on the sidewalk in downtown New York City and make the primary, "I am happy," and you will be happy. Or you could make the primary, "This is beautiful," and you will see beauty all around. But if you make the primary, "I am in Chicago," you probably won't suddenly transport a thousand miles to Chicago. Teleportation is not within your primary's power—not yet.

Convincing yourself that you are in Chicago

while you are still in New York is delusional thinking. There is plenty of that. You can find dozens of street derelicts who have convinced themselves of primaries that are in complete disagreement with the reality in which they are living. The back pressure from making a primary that can't manifest is a delusional reality. (Mental hospitals are filled with people who are living and creating in delusional realities.)

Rationally, there are two choices you can make with the primary, "I am in Chicago." One, you can let the primary highlight a path of opportunity— for example, you notice there is a bus terminal on the corner—or you can redirect the primary to change your mental state and handle self-limitations. For example, "I want to go to Chicago, and there is nothing stopping me."

Primaries work best when they are used to shape and steer the reality in which you are operating, rather than challenging the limits of that reality.

Making the primary, "I am an expert sky diver," and then wondering why your parachute doesn't open while you plummet to Earth is a difficult secondary to exaggerate. Expert sky diver was a delusional reality, which you will convincingly discover when your body impacts the Earth.

It's an unwise concession to the ego to primary a skill that you haven't confidently achieved by study and practice. What you can primary is the mental perseverance to acquire the skill. Skills are acquired by study (including contemplation and observation) and practice. The perseverance to study and practice is the result of primaries. The correct primary is, "I will study and practice sky diving until I become an expert."

By contrast, sky diving is a no-brainer compared to the study and practice required to become a successful Avatar Master. Making the primary, "I am a successful Avatar Master" may be satisfying to the ego, but it is the wrong primary. It is delusional. The impact that will convince you that it is delusional is called poverty!

Consider a first-year medical student who makes the primary, "I am an expert surgeon." Are you going to let him or her operate on you?

The right primary is, "I will practice and study until I become a successful Avatar Master." Voila!

Here are some of the skills you need to acquire to succeed as a Master:

- contact skills
- communication skills
- listening and observation skills
- marketing skills
- sales skills
- management skills
- teaching skills
- bookkeeping skills

There is a difference between a mental state and a skill. It's easy to primary a mental state, but it is a little delusional to think you can primary a skill. (How to acquire a skill—it's easier than you think—is discussed in Chapter 4.)

Trainer's Nightmare

Somewhere a new Master comes home from the Master Course and decides to deliver Avatar. He makes the primary, "I have ten new Avatar students."

The phone rings, and a friend invites him to a party. (Hint: path of opportunity.) No, he can't go. He has to work on his primary, "I have ten new Avatar students." A neighbor drops by to chat.

(Hint: path of opportunity.) "Can't talk now. I have to work on my primary."

The date for the course comes (and goes) and no one signs up. "Primaries don't work for me," he grumbles.

Somewhere Star's Edge Trainers toss restlessly in their sleep. Aaa-r-r-g!

Recognizing Opportunity

There is a story about a man who is trapped on a roof by rising flood waters. He prays, "God will save me."

Rescuers in a boat come by, but he refuses to get in. "It would be a weakness in my faith," he tells them. "God will save me." The waters continue to rise. Finally a Coast Guard helicopter comes and hovers overhead. He refuses to climb the ladder. "It would be a weakness in my faith. God will save me." The waters finally rise over the roof, and he is swept away and drowns.

When he reaches Heaven, he cries out angrily to God. "I kept my faith. Why didn't you answer my prayers?"

God replies, "Answer your prayers? I sent a boat and a helicopter. What more did you want?"

The Right Way

New Masters can either recognize the paths of opportunity that are highlighted by their primaries, or they can redirect their primaries into the universe of self to remove self-limitations. For example, "I will practice connecting with people at least two hours a day and sell them books about Avatar."

It's a little long for a primary, but it is the one that will produce the result.

Some Masters rely on a primary like, "Everyone (or a person's name) wants to read *Living Deliberately*." It is probably safe to say that this primary exerts an intentional pressure on people to buy and read the book. But even more importantly, it removes self-defeating secondaries in the seller.

Be, Do, and Have Primaries

Primaries directly affect being and doing. When a having is primaried, a path of being and doing will reveal itself that, if followed, will eventually arrive at having the thing.

If you want immediate gratification, primary states of being (e.g. being happy). Being is not stained by the world. You can create any state of being and any feeling. Deliberately creating different states tames the mind. Quick rewards.

If you are willing to temporarily delay gratification, primary both being and doing. These primaries will involve some effort, but getting out and around is wonderfully therapeutic.

Primaries and Magic

Putting a primary in someone else's universe has some consequences you had better know about. When you act as a hidden influence on another, you are also making yourself susceptible to hidden influences.

These are advanced techniques that are best left to Wizards.

Primaries and Domains
(from a 1997 Wizard lecture)

A domain is a sphere or area of activity. It's an area for which you assume some responsibility and in which you have some influence. There are physical domains and consciousness domains. We are going to start by talking about physical domains.

Similar domains, by definition, are in the same range of magnitude, such as farms in a valley. Each farm is the domain of one farmer who works the farm and makes the decisions about plantings and harvests. The farmer assumes some responsibility for the farm and has some influence on what is grown or produced.

The farmer may have employees who work in his domain, but they have lesser amounts of influence. You could create a scale of the influence each participant has in a particular domain. For instance, the farmer is the boss and makes the major decisions, the farm foreman gives orders to the workers, and the workers do what they are told. We are describing three levels of participation in this domain. The farmer, the foreman, and the workers are all operating in the same domain, but they each have different powers of influence over the events in that domain.

You could change domain. Say the foreman has his own farm, and the first farmer goes to help with the foreman's harvest. The farmer, moving from the domain of his farm to the domain of the foreman's farm, changes his role. He goes from being the boss to being the worker.

The two farms are domains in the same range of magnitude. We could call them family farms.

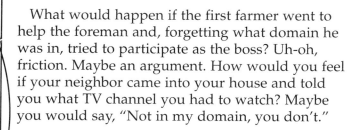

What would happen if the first farmer went to help the foreman and, forgetting what domain he was in, tried to participate as the boss? Uh-oh, friction. Maybe an argument. How would you feel if your neighbor came into your house and told you what TV channel you had to watch? Maybe you would say, "Not in my domain, you don't."

The participants in a domain work out their own right-to-influence scale. It may be arrived at by competition, as it is in nature, or it may be arrived at by agreement, as it is, ideally, among friends. There are also chance ways of establishing right-to-influence scales such as the flip of a coin.

You could call any of these right-to-influence scales the politics of the domain. Anytime you have a domain with more than one participant, you are going to have politics.

There are also domains of different magnitude.

Domains in the same order of magnitude often form collectives. The collective, taken as a whole, is a domain of greater magnitude. The president of the farmer's cooperative operates in a domain of greater magnitude than that of the farmer.

So we've got two ideas here. We have the idea of influential power within a domain, and we have the idea of different magnitudes of domains.

In the domain of the bow and arrow, the best archer had the most influence. However, when he stumbled into the domain of the cannon, he quickly lost his influence. The cannon is a different magnitude of domain.

Another example of a domain in a different order of magnitude is the county or the province in which our farms exist. The reason we call a county or province a different order of magnitude is not just because of its size—you could have a farm the size of a county. The real difference is in the magnitude of influence. A county commissioner has a greater magnitude of power to influence events than a farmer has.

The next higher level of domain might be the state in which the county is located. Again, this is a change in order of magnitude. The state governor has greater magnitude of influence than a county commissioner has.

You not only have a pecking order within a domain, but you actually have a pecking order of magnitudes of domains.

Even though the governor is the political boss in the domain of the state, and the farmer is the political boss in the domain of the farm, they have different magnitudes of influence.

The president of the country has more power to influence than the governor of the state has, because the country is a domain of greater magnitude than the state.

If the farmer looks across the valley and makes the primary, "I'm going to build a hydroelectric dam," what's going to happen? The other farmers are going to object. His neighbors are going to turn into secondaries. He doesn't really have the power to create that primary, because it's outside his domain. He's going to have to work very hard to handle his neighbors' secondaries.

The governor can look across the same valley and make the primary, "I'm going to build a hydroelectric dam." Some farmers may object to having their land flooded, but he is the governor and their objections are just very small secondaries. He does, *and now the primary* a few times, pays the farmers off or throws them in jail—he doesn't need

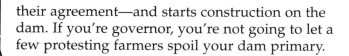

their agreement—and starts construction on the dam. If you're governor, you're not going to let a few protesting farmers spoil your dam primary.

Unfortunately, the valley the governor picked to build a dam is one of the favorite vacation spots of the president. Suddenly the governor finds an executive order on his desk halting construction on the dam. This dam secondary is coming from the president who operates in a greater domain.

Have you ever tried to make a primary and run into secondaries from a domain that is a magnitude above the domain you are operating in?

Have you ever had an Avatar student complain because his primary to win the lottery didn't work? You see, he's on the farm, and he's trying to run the country.

I once had a student ask me if I could levitate. I had to say no. What I should have said was, "Do you have the power to declare war on Canada?"

If you make the primary, "When I drop my pencil it will fall to the ceiling," what's going to happen? A secondary called gravity.

It's not a matter of faith that your pencil doesn't fall upward. It's a violation of the rules of a greater domain than the one in which you are operating. Again, you're trying to issue a presidential order from the domain of the farmer. It's like saying to the hired man, "Plant the oats, feed the chickens, and then balance the national budget." Different domains!

I think it would be safe, at least for now, to say that every domain defines a sphere in which you have the freedom to create, but also defines the limits of your creating. Learning the freedoms and limits of the domain you are operating in is called living.

When you repeatedly come up against the limits of the domain you are operating in—meaning your primaries are overwhelmed by secondaries from a more powerful domain—it is time to move up an order of magnitude. Time to play a bigger game.

Chapter 4

Building Skills

There are beingness scales described in the Pro Course and Wizard materials. What follows here is a doingness scale. It measures a being's performance in regard to a specific skill or skill package. It should be noted at the beginning that a person may be found at one level in regard to one skill and at another level in regard to a different skill. —HP

Skill building adds a new dimension to work. Normally, you determine the success or failure of working by the product that is produced. In a society that is heavily focused on immediate gratification, if the work doesn't immediately produce a successful product, people tend to give up the effort and move on. Actually, they move down, because people very rarely tackle a job that is tougher than the one they fail out of.

Allowing yourself a period of self-directed internship turns mistakes and failures into discoveries rather than blows to your self-esteem. Interning is a hands-on learning experience that has the purpose of building skills. Interns are expected to make mistakes and not produce very much for their efforts, but they learn. The real struggle for an intern is not to give in to discouragement or to be seduced into easier paths.

The effort needed to produce the same or better results decreases as you acquire skill. This ratio of effort to results is really a measure of performance. You can call this a performance scale. There are distinct performance levels that you pass through when engaging in any enterprise (including evolution).

To use this scale, determine your current situation and follow the program given for that level to improve your performance to the next level.

0. Confusion

Situation: Uncertainty as to what effort will produce a result. Waiting for something to happen. Priorities and importances are unclear. Attention wanders. No production.

PROGRAM: UNDERTAKE SOMETHING. MAKE YOUR INTENTIONS KNOWN TO ASSOCIATES.

1. Struggle

Situation: There are obstructions (secondaries). Effort is expended, but there is very little progress and no finished product. It feels like a good time to give up and try something else.

PROGRAM: FIND SOMEONE WHO IS PRODUCING A RESULT AND STUDY HOW IT IS PRODUCED (SEEK A MASTER). FAILING TO FIND A MASTER, PRIMARY THE SELF-DISCIPLINE FOR TRIAL-AND-ERROR RESEARCH.

2. First Results

Situation: A discouraging amount of effort is required to repeat difficult steps, to cope, and to backtrack and re-do procedures, but in the end a small quantity of results is produced.

PROGRAM: DIVIDE THE TASK INTO STEPS OR STAGES THAT CAN BE ORDERED, REPEATED, AND PRACTICED.

3. Frustration

Situation: There is a dip in performance. It

worked. Now it doesn't. Results seem to be produced more by chance than by design or effort. What's causing or obstructing results isn't clear.

PROGRAM: BACK UP AND REVIEW. SLOW DOWN. HANDLE TRANSPARENT BELIEFS. SURRENDER JUDGMENTS, AND DISCOVER WHAT REALLY WORKED.

4. Routine Performance

Situation: A certain amount of effort produces a certain amount of result. Connection between effort and result may not be apparent.

PROGRAM: CONTINUE TO WORK HARD. ESTABLISH A RESOURCE BASE. FOCUS ADDITIONAL ENERGY INTO EFFORTS THAT WILL PRODUCE RESULTS OVER THE LONG TERM. ASSIST OTHERS.

5. Confidence

Situation: Attention is available for handling details. Quantity stabilizes or continues to increase while quality improves. Production becomes an art. A momentum is achieved. A reliable result can be produced by tapping the momentum.

PROGRAM: ASSUME GREATER RESPONSIBILITY. REPAIR FAULTY PRODUCTS. RECOGNIZE OR DEFINE SUB-PRODUCTS. INCREASE PRODUCTIVE EFFORTS AND ELIMINATE UNPRODUCTIVE EFFORTS. ALIGN WITH AND EMPOWER TEAMMATES.

6. Authority (Leadership)

Situation: Production increases as the result of good management. Maturity.

PROGRAM: STANDARDIZE AND DOCUMENT PROCEDURES. TRAIN AND SUPERVISE. ORGANIZE.

Delegate tasks and authority. Create a self-sustaining organization with vision.

7. Enlightenment

Situation: Such an absence of external restriction and limitation that it depends only upon the inward determination of the subject whether or not it will act. (This state is called power in the Wizard materials.)

Program: Selfless service to others. Look to intuitive guidance.

(Note: This scale and the programs apply to whole projects, partnerships, companies, governments, and civilizations, as well as to individual skills.)

Introduction to Performance Scale

If you want to raise your performance level, which means getting a better result in both quality and quantity of product, you have to move up on this scale. Determine honestly the situation you are in—not the situation you wish you were in or the situation you'd like others to believe you are in, but the actual situation you are in regarding the job, project, or task you have undertaken. Following the program for that level will move you upward on the scale. (Following a program for a level of performance you have not reached will cause damage and wind you down into confusion.)

Confusion and enlightenment are the only states that will sustain themselves without any effort. They are the entrance and the exit to a domain. It is **confusion** to imagine that they are the same.

Following all of the program steps will eventually lead you through an entire domain into the next larger domain. Failing the steps and lacking enough discipline to persevere will lead you back into lesser domains. The three major domains across which human evolution treks are animal, intellectual, and spiritual. Within these major domains are minor domains (survival, projects, jobs, family, consciousness) that you must cross.

Confusion

PROGRAM: UNDERTAKE SOMETHING. MAKE YOUR INTENTIONS KNOWN TO ASSOCIATES.

Confusion always exists just beyond the limits of your comfort zone. Boundaries, property lines, and walls are motivated by an effort to keep confusion out. People have different capacities to endure confusion. Some people find it interesting; some find it fearfully painful. People who confront confusion can expand and acquire new skills. People who won't confront confusion will panic and seek a contracted domain. Introversion, apathy, acceptance of failure are the result of too much avoidance of confusion.

Confusion that is resisted too strongly is actually projected into the environment in the form of irresponsible, even criminal, acts.

If you resist something with enough force, you project it into the environment and are surrounded by it. —Wizard lecture

Predictability of cause-and-effect relationships approaches zero in a state of confusion. Imagine you are in a room with hundreds of switches, buttons, and levers. An ominous clock is counting down. A rising amplitude of screams. Something is going to happen. Time is running out. What do you do? You can give up or you can try something.

What you try may not work, but at least you are making progress. The confusion will begin to subside as you learn what doesn't work. Famous inventor of the light bulb, Thomas Edison, after a year of failure, is quoted as saying, "I've discovered ten thousand things that don't work."

In the moment you try something, you enter the level of struggle.

Struggle

PROGRAM: FIND SOMEONE WHO IS PRODUCING A RESULT AND STUDY HOW IT IS PRODUCED (SEEK A MASTER). FAILING TO FIND A MASTER, PRIMARY THE SELF-DISCIPLINE FOR TRIAL-AND-ERROR RESEARCH.

From a positive viewpoint, struggle is sorting out a confusion by the elimination of what doesn't work. It's a learning situation rather than a productive situation.

Struggle proceeds like this. You discover what doesn't work and begin to get an idea of what is obstructing you. Maybe you aren't making any headway in interesting people in Avatar. No book sales. No prospects. No students. But you are discovering your own limitations and are focusing in on the obstruction. How long will you struggle? Will you give up or will you keep trying?

If you wish to accelerate your progress through this struggle stage, find a Master who is contacting, connecting, and registering Avatar students and study how he or she is doing it. Even better, make arrangements to intern with the Master—not just during a delivery, but volunteer to help between deliveries.

If you can't find a qualified Master to study or intern with, study this manual. Or, if you are engaged in a task for which there is no manual, roll up your sleeves and proceed on a trial-and-error basis until you produce your first result. Primary: "I will keep learning and trying until I succeed."

First Results

PROGRAM: DIVIDE THE TASK INTO STEPS OR STAGES THAT CAN BE ORDERED, REPEATED, AND PRACTICED.

First results are causes for celebration. They are also a signal that the real work still lies ahead. Continuing beyond first results is what separates the dilettantes from the professionals.

At this level you have concentrated enough effort into the correct actions to produce a result. Unfortunately, unless your Master was a very good teacher, the correct actions are sprinkled among a lot of incorrect and unnecessary actions. But you have moved up from the level of struggle where there were no successful results. You now know that if you are willing to put in enough effort, you can produce a result, e.g., you sell a book to a stranger, but it took 30 tries.

The good news is that you know it can be done. The bad news is that this is probably not the toughest sale you'll ever make. Why? Because you don't know exactly why you succeeded.

How did you do it? What worked? What steps were involved? At this stage, the solution is to duplicate exactly what you did before. Divide what you did into steps that you can practice. Have a friend coach you.

The next thing that happens is a bit of a mystery to some people and is the reason why so many fail—your technique stops working.

Frustration

PROGRAM: BACK UP AND REVIEW. SLOW DOWN.
HANDLE TRANSPARENT BELIEFS. SURRENDER
JUDGMENTS, AND DISCOVER WHAT REALLY WORKED.

Discouragement is giving up **before** you know
you can get a result. Frustration is failing **after** you
know you can get a result.

The truth is that first results are often more a
matter of luck than of skill. You just happen to tell
the right person about your ailing mother curing
herself with Avatar, and they bought a book. The
next 150 people you tell your ailing-mother success
story to not only don't buy a book, they begin
avoiding you.

Now you are at the level of frustration which, if
viewed positively, is really a very interesting level
of discovery and realization. Frustration is a signal
that you are on the path to a breakthrough
realization, e.g., doing more of what doesn't work
doesn't work. Slow down.

You discover you have some transparent beliefs
about the importance of an endorsement by
mother and that you are actually showing some
antagonism toward people who don't share your
beliefs. Your Serious Drill has succumbed to
frustration. Okay, so you get that out of the way.
Now what really worked?

You learn by a little investigation that the person
you sold the book to also has an ailing mother.
Your story was relevant. They perceived the book
as offering a possible solution to a situation they
had. That's what really worked; you struck a chord
and they resonated. Aha! Realization.

Now you know that if you invest the time and
effort to find out what situation a person has

attention stuck on, and your offer is recognized as a possible solution to that situation, you sell books.

You have just reached the level where a certain amount of effort on your part will produce a certain amount of result.

Routine Performance

PROGRAM: CONTINUE TO WORK HARD. ESTABLISH A RESOURCE BASE. FOCUS ADDITIONAL ENERGY INTO EFFORTS THAT WILL PRODUCE RESULTS OVER THE LONG TERM. ASSIST OTHERS.

When something becomes routine, there is a human tendency to minimize the effort that is expended. Sometimes a person rationalizes that they are practicing efficiency, but the efficiency is really laziness and results in a decline of results. At this level, a certain amount of effort produces a certain amount of result. If you reduce your efforts, you will likely reduce your results.

Sometimes new Masters go home, and they are all practiced up from the Master Course. They talk to strangers in the airport about Avatar. They make primaries, do the Discouragement Drill, sell books to their friends and maybe even at the local flea market or health food store. They expend a lot of effort disseminating Avatar, but nothing happens immediately. Maybe they are just a little short of the amount of effort needed to produce a result. Then they run a small classified ad offering Avatar, and two people call up and come in for the course. Wow!

So the next month they don't bother with making new contacts, or primaries, or book sales, but, because they're easy and inexpensive, they run four classified ads. What happens?

You guessed it, nothing happens. No calls, no sign-ups. From their point of view, it seems that students show up more by chance than from anything they are doing. Getting Avatar students appears to be more a matter of luck than the result of efforts. Maybe they wonder if they need a better ad.

Guess what? They have just slid back down into the level of frustration. If they are clever, they will immediately re-apply the solution for frustration.

What influenced the students to sign up? They do a little investigation. They discover that one student had heard about Avatar from a Master in a gym two years ago. The student then received an *Avatar Journal* and bought *Living Deliberately*, but never read them. The student's friend called from California and happened to mention that a mutual acquaintance of theirs was doing a course called Avatar, so the student read the book and made a mental note that it was something that she'd like to do someday. Then the student saw the classified ad, but she didn't immediately call. Instead, she called the acquaintance who was doing Avatar and said she was thinking about doing Avatar. The acquaintance raved about her Avatar experience and appeared to be happier than the student remembered her. The student then called the new Master and signed up.

So, it wasn't magic after all. It was an accumulations of efforts (causes) that finally influenced the student to do Avatar. The classified ad was only the final trigger of a successful contact effort, a more information effort, a successful book sales effort, and the testimonial of a satisfied Avatar graduate effort that finally paid off. Realization! A certain amount of effort produces a certain amount of result. The Master goes to work and climbs back to the level of routine performance.

This time they will succeed, because they see the bigger picture. They realize that every Master's productive efforts feed into a large energy pool that is awakening people to Avatar. This is what is meant by *establish a resource base.* Creating an enlightened planetary civilization is a shared undertaking. A certain amount of effort produces a certain amount of result. Maybe none of the people to whom they disseminate information will sign up, but they are not failing. Their efforts are feeding into a much larger cause-and-effect resource base. You have to adopt an expanded viewpoint to see this.

A Master in Singapore disseminates to doctors, a Master in New York disseminates to massage therapists. What happens? Neither gets any sign-ups. However, a New York massage therapist vacations in Singapore and does Avatar with the Singapore Master. A doctor who was in Singapore returns to New York and does Avatar with the New York Master. In both cases, their efforts have produced a result. A certain amount of effort produces a certain amount of result.

The energy pool into which each of these Masters is directing productive efforts is the resource base. The more productive effort they flow into it, the more results they will get—**even when there is no obvious connection between their efforts and their results.**

How much effort it takes to get a result is determined by how productive the effort is. Some Masters' efforts are more productive and feed more energy into the pool. Typically, they get more results. Some Masters' efforts are minimal and not very productive. They do not feed much energy into the pool and do not get many results. They give up in frustration.

People who understand this level of performance are destined for success. The people who fail to grasp it are destined for repeated failings and frustration.

When you hear some inexperienced Masters complain that there are too many Masters and too much competition, just recognize that they don't have a clue about how this level of performance operates.

Confidence

PROGRAM: ASSUME GREATER RESPONSIBILITY. REPAIR FAULTY PRODUCTS. RECOGNIZE OR DEFINE SUB-PRODUCTS. INCREASE PRODUCTIVE EFFORTS AND ELIMINATE UNPRODUCTIVE EFFORTS. ALIGN WITH AND EMPOWER TEAMMATES.

The level of confidence discussed here means an ability to demonstrate competence. It is reached after a sustained period of routine performance (hard work). It is not empty arrogance. It is ability. It is achieved when you know how to produce results.

As you gain confidence, competition transforms naturally into cooperation. (There is nothing to prove, and no one needs to fail for you to succeed.)

If a deep affection for the work and for teammates has not surfaced by this time, you are probably in the wrong profession. Do a Right-For-You (RFY) goal program.

At this level, quality, in both dissemination and delivery, is improved. If past errors exist, they are rectified. Productive actions are organized according to the sub-products produced. Sub-products become a ladder to the final result.

The efforts necessary to produce sub-products are systematized and practiced until they become automatic. Efficiency of effort is achieved by sorting the productive efforts from the unproductive ones, without lowering the quantity or quality of result.

People who are confident in their abilities derive satisfaction from working in specialized teams. A confident team is very powerful.

Authority (Leadership)

PROGRAM: STANDARDIZE AND DOCUMENT PROCEDURES. TRAIN AND SUPERVISE. ORGANIZE. DELEGATE TASKS AND AUTHORITY. CREATE A SELF-SUSTAINING ORGANIZATION WITH VISION.

Leaders come in many varieties. The most dangerous leaders are those who are appointed or elected for reasons other than their ability to produce the expected products or the results of the enterprise. The best leaders, also the rarest, obtain authority as a result of their competence.

When a leadership post is first established, it is almost always established because of a crisis. The pressure from a backlog of decisions that need to be made, orders that need to be given, or enemies that need to be neutralized has grown greater than individual efforts can handle. Founding leaders have to be very familiar with the situations and resources of their group. Very familiar. There isn't time for committees or fact-finding investigations. They had better have an answer, solution, or program ready to go. Otherwise the group's empowerment can quickly change into a sacrificial ceremony.

Don't even dream of assuming leadership in a crisis unless you have a sustained period of confident performance under your belt. You won't believe the speed with which an adoring group can turn into a lynch mob. Even when you assume an established post of leadership that is running smoothly, if you haven't come up through the levels of this scale you are at high risk.

If a leader wishes to enjoy the same life span as the average person, he or she will expediently create and/or empower an organization that operates according to the most efficient policy that can be gleaned from both personal experience and the group's history. Organizations may be unpopular with unaligned individuals, but they are crucial to the well-being of a leader. Creating the organization around an aligning vision creates a stable reference point for decisions not covered by policy (e.g., contributing to the creation of an enlightened planetary civilization or upholding a national constitution).

Enlightenment

PROGRAM: SELFLESS SERVICE TO OTHERS. LOOK TO INTUITIVE GUIDANCE.

Not every leader reaches enlightenment. In fact, most leaders never rise above the performance level of frustration. But for the real leader who has honestly worked his or her way through this scale, enlightenment comes naturally.

Real service to others requires discernment and some ability to foresee consequences—wisdom. Real service is ultimately empowering **to all**. Thus, helping someone commit a destructive act against another is not service. Making someone dependent upon you is probably not service. Filling someone's head with commanding or limiting beliefs is probably not service. Many actions, though apparently kindly intended, are probably not real service to others.

As you ascend this scale, there will be many reasons and opportunities to serve others in mutually empowering ways. Serving others is the best way to accomplish your own ends. Serving others is satisfying. Serving others is admired. Serving others is charitable. All real service to others, for whatever reason it is given, is a contribution to an enlightened planetary civilization.

At this level of enlightenment, the character of service to others changes. It becomes service to the ONE. There is no self advantage in serving others. There is no self. Being has awakened in an awareness that is deeper than any self need or conscious definition.

Chapter 5

Avatar Master Identity

Before you start thinking about dissemination, think about yourself as a role model. How skilled a representative of Avatar are you? What kind of example are you setting? People spontaneously imitate each other. If someone imitates you, will they be a step closer to living in an enlightened planetary civilization or a step further away? What if everyone in the world imitated you?

Do you offer the world an easy-to-imitate model for acquiring and practicing wisdom? Make your identity the first contribution you make to an enlightened planetary civilization.

For people who are new to Avatar, you are the first impression they have of Avatar. This spontaneous mental image that they call (insert your name) will either become good feelings about Avatar or it will become a secondary in their mind to any future mention of Avatar.

Now here is a great secret: the best impression you can make on someone is to let them make a good impression on you. How do you do that? You accept them. You make space for them. You are reserved but have an abundant amount of patient attention to listen with interest. It's more important to discover who they are being than to tell them who you are being.

When you speak, your stories and words should be chosen to amuse, inform, or inspire others rather than to impress them with some asserted self-definition. Leave them remembering what was said rather than who said it.

Appearance is only skin deep, but that doesn't mean that it doesn't make a first impression. It does. Be clean and well groomed. Create characteristics that are easy to identify with: modest confidence, helpfulness, consideration, acceptance, friendliness. Dress neatly and conventionally—unless your deliberate intention is to attract attention.

Expecting another person to look beyond the physical surface you are presenting is asking for something. That's not offering a role model of Avatar. Are there some personal issues around seeking recognition or asserting importance that you need to address? What is the first impression that people have of you? How are they getting it? What first impression do you want them to have of you? Why?

Your deliberate identity and practiced manners are like a menu in a restaurant window. They either turn people who are curious into customers or they turn them away. Testing and developing a positive body language can be the difference between success and failure.

The most important contribution you make to an enlightened planetary civilization is the example you set by how you live your own life. Be a role model.

If you have experienced a lot of rejection in your life and have trouble meeting people, it is time to take a personal inventory of exactly how you are coming across to the other person. A Star's Edge Trainer or a courageous friend can help you if you're bold enough to ask. Are you neat and clean in appearance? Is your body language appropriate for an introduction? Are you making some statement with your attitude or style of dress? Are you making a nonverbal request or demand for recognition from the other person? Are you making facial gestures that are challenging to a person's status or opinion? Is your attention on the person you are meeting or on yourself? Are you really looking through your own eyes or are you imagining what they are seeing through their eyes? Are you seeking approval or validation?

The answers to these questions may jolt you, but they also provide a starting point for your deliberate transformation. Remember, the more closely associated you are with a creation, the less visible it becomes.

Qualities Worth Nurturing

wisdom the power or faculty of forming the fittest and truest judgment in any matter presented for consideration; a knowledge of people and things gained by experience

judgment the determination of the degree of alignment or misalignment of something with the ideal

discernment the faculty of distinguishing the essential differences

discretion the ability to avoid mistakes; to separate aligned actions from misaligned actions; selecting the best means to accomplish a purpose

sagacious keenly perceptive, discerning, of human motives and actions

sincerity being real, without pretense or secondaries

humanity consideration for the sensibilities of others and sympathy with their needs or suffering; kindness; a disposition to relieve distress, whether of humans or animals, and to treat all creatures kindly

courage the quality of mind that enables one to encounter danger and difficulties without fear or depression ...*and now the primary*

Right Conduct

Avatar cuts across so many nations and so many cultures that it is not possible to describe a detailed code of conduct for Avatar Masters. What is offered here are generalized observations.

Right conduct is satisfying your basic needs in a deliberate way that does not lead to future condemnation or regret. (The Buddhist would say no karma is incurred.)

Right conduct does not threaten anyone else's basic needs (present or future).

Right conduct communicates a recognition and respect for the other.

Right conduct is a gift of opportunity to others.

Impulse and the Deliberate Will

Whenever possible, act with a plan to create or improve conditions (a primary) rather than from an impulse to acquire or resist something. Acting on impulse is a futile effort and is not the same as acting spontaneously or intuitively as source.

An impulse is not a rational action. It is an imbalance that arises from an unexplored region of consciousness—a secondary to some substance, person, or event. It rises like the waves of a storm and, if allowed, will sweep away the deliberate will. Any action for which you later feel a need to rationalize is probably done out of impulse.

The way you handle an impulse is to steer into the storm. Hunker down into your being. Be still. Do nothing. Feel it and let it pass without reacting. It will wash over you and eventually disappear. Nothing can wash away your being.

If the situation allows and you know and want to create the primary that caused the secondary impulse, you can speed up things with the Section II Creation Exercise.

Whew! ...*and now the primary.*

Masters Who Hear Confessions

On occasion, circumstances may dictate that an Avatar Master hear someone's confession. At such times, the Master should strictly observe non-judgment.

An Avatar Master should hear a confession only if it is motivated by repentance. Therefore the first question is always, "Do you repent your actions and wish to change your ways?"

The only coaxing allowed is, "Is that all you want to tell me?" **NOT** "Is there anything else you want to tell me?"

The Avatar Master ends the confession with, "Thank you for your honesty. Will you pledge to do everything you can to make up the damage your actions have caused?"

A repentant confession is confidential.

Your Business Being

Depending upon your locale, there are certain legal obligations to running a business, e.g., keeping income and expense records, tax matters, registration of business name, zoning requirements, opening banking accounts, making arrangements to accept credit cards, etc. You can do your own research by talking to other business people, or you can consult a local accountant. Many libraries as well as bookstores, carry books on how to start a small business.

Your business being is created after a period of operation. No one honestly expects a person who is starting a business to be immediately in compliance with every regulation, but this is an area where you should continue to make steady progress.

Your Core Business

Concentrate on satisfying the self-discovery, self-recovery, and self-realization needs of your students.

Primaries In Conflict (Arguments)

Presuming to express another's motives (or their viewpoint) in a conflict is a grave error. Until some peace is restored, drop the use of all forms of the word **you**. Listen. Ask questions, but not in an interrogating tone. The appropriate questions are those that will clarify your understanding, not their understanding. Unless you are in the role of a superior or a counselor, don't question people toward their realization of something. Stay in your own mind. Listen.

Determination is a quality of the heart and mind. It should not be profaned by stubborn words or demands.

Sincere manners and respectful questioning open paths of opportunity that many would miss. Making friends with an adversary can lead to a co-intuitive compromise that was not visible or possible in the absence of the friendship. When a genuine friendship is established, conflicts melt into cooperative efforts.

Where is That Waitress?

It is easy when you are tired and stressed to slip into a victim viewpoint. Sometimes it seems that the service, or other people's outright neglect of you, is so unfair that your only option is to scream, "Do you have any idea who I am?"

This is not a good idea. The eventual result of a display of self-importance is humiliation. A much better approach is to rapidly discreate your resentment and to observe the other person. What is their attention on? What's troubling them? What's going on behind the scenes? Is there something that you can do to be helpful without being intrusive? Is your patience helpful?

Compassion and consideration, even when they do not seem to have an effect on the other, release healing and calming forces in your own body.

Relevant Information, Proper Acknowledgment, Sincere Appreciation and Genuine Admiration

Amazingly, these four abstract commodities are apparently considered more valuable by the current civilization than any other thing, including health, wealth, and power. They are the fundamental incentives that motivate people to better themselves, to perform better, and to strive for higher goals. They are the secret desires that fuel human consciousness.

Probably the reason they drive people so hard is because they are in such short supply. (By analogy, if everyone wanted to eat bread, but there were no bakers, bread would become very valuable.) But why are relevant information, proper acknowledgment, sincere appreciation, and genuine admiration in such short supply in the current civilization?

It's not really that much of a mystery. The majority of the population are absorbed in calculating how to receive (get) these commodities from others. Calculating how to get them is service to self. Calculating how to get them does not produce them, but merely adds to the demand that already far exceeds the current supply.

You are Masters because you have tapped into an abundant supply of these abstract, yet priceless, commodities. You give them away. You calculate how to give more away. Your work is giving them away. And the more you give away, the more abundant your own supply becomes. That is another secret.

Section II

Building Momentum

The commitment to something beyond self interest
is a cry from a soul that has been awakened.

Inamori, Japanese CEO

Chapter 6

Productive Efforts

Whacking at the Beast

Your efforts are like water filling a basin. When the water gets deep enough, it will flow in some direction. An awful lot of effort seems to go nowhere, but it helps to fill the basin.

Masters who have been around for awhile have all heard the phrase "whacking at the beast." It means to keep making progress doing whatever you can do.

A good explanation of whacking at the beast is discovered by putting together a large jigsaw puzzle. There are so many different-colored pieces that the idea of completing the puzzle is quite overwhelming, so you just concentrate on what you can do. Here are two yellow pieces that fit together. Here is an upper corner. You place that where it will eventually fit. You start collecting the pieces of sky into a pile. There is another yellow piece. And you just keep whacking at the beast. Eventually, just by doing whatever you can do, the puzzle is completed.

If you tried to do the same puzzle by always looking for a specific piece, instead of just doing whatever you can do, it would take much longer and you'd probably succumb to overwhelm before the puzzle was done. So whacking at the beast has this element of doing whatever it is that you can do in the moment.

Sub-Products

Oftentimes there are multiple sub-products involved in achieving a final product. This is quite obvious in manufacturing where several different companies may be involved in producing sub-assemblies that are finally assembled into a finished product at the main plant, e.g., an automobile.

The sub-products involved in delivering a service, such as an Avatar Course, are not always so obvious, but they exist nonetheless. Understanding what they are can help you to determine whether or not your efforts are productive, i.e., if they are turning a resource into a sub-product.

Each successful sub-product that you produce brings someone closer to being an Avatar graduate.

Sub-Product Table

RESOURCE	EFFORT	SUB-PRODUCT
1. A person who has never heard of Avatar.	First contact	A person who knows that Avatar is a course about learning to live deliberately.
2. A person who has heard of Avatar (good or bad).	Expose them to the actual testimonials of people who have completed Avatar.	A person who knows that people have benefited greatly from Avatar.
3. A person who has heard something favorable about Avatar.	Align the benefits of Avatar with a personal need, a goal, or with resolving a personal situation.	A person who has a hunch that Avatar might offer some personal benefits and is seeking more information.
4. A person who has some interest in Avatar.	Sell them an Avatar book or tape and/or get their name and address for an *Avatar Journal*.	A person who possesses accurate information about Avatar. Someone who has tested it out mentally.
5. A person who owns an Avatar book, tape or tape set.	Involve and inspire. Has the material been read? What did they think? Encourage them to apply the ideas in their own thinking.	A person who would like to experience an Avatar process and understand themselves better (a friend of Avatar).
6. Avatar prospect	Get them to an experiential Avatar event that stimulates realizations about life. Describe the expected results of Avatar.	A person who has tested some elementary Avatar techniques with good results and has moved doing Avatar to the top of his or her priority list.
7. Pre-Avatar student	Present the agenda for the course. Assist them to register and arrive.	An Avatar student
8. An enrolled student	Deliver Avatar professionally and compassionately to the expected results.	An Avatar student making progress and having major life wins and realizations.
9. A happy Avatar student	Get a call list of people who might be interested in Avatar.	An aligned Avatar graduate and future Avatar prospects.

Expect Instant Success,
But Have a Back Up Plan

It is too bad that the information contained in this chapter was not available sooner. It would have given direction to a lot of Masters who didn't know where to start and saved other Masters who gave up when they were on the verge of success. Count yourself fortunate to now have a clear road map of the efforts and sub-products that lead to success.

Every person in your Rolodex or database is at some level of resource in this sub-product table. As an exercise, you might want to sort through your names and assign them a number from one to nine according to the category of resource they are.

If you find that the majority of your people fall into one resource category, you can conclude that there is some difficulty in performing the effort to the immediate right of that category. Maybe it is a skill you will have to learn (see Chapter 4), or maybe it's just an effort you have to incorporate into your repertoire.

Your job is to know the type of resource a person is and to successfully process him or her to the next stage of completed sub-product. The processes consist of connecting, listening, chatting, encouraging, and course delivery. These are the combined efforts that move a person who has never heard of Avatar through the stages of sub-products to become an Avatar graduate.

Always concentrate on the effort needed to transform the person you happen to be talking with into the next sub-product stage. (Reference: "Whacking At The Beast"). Some people will move from being a number one resource to a number eight resource very rapidly. Others may take four or five years before they become a number eight resource. An unfortunate few will not realize the opportunity they missed.

Effort #1: Friendly Relations

Avatar has always expanded by word of mouth—sincere honesty, friend to friend. That's more than a successful marketing strategy. It is the foundation of the civilization that we are creating. It is the core of the practice of Avatar. Masters who believe everything would be solved with a massive media campaign are frustrated in the friend-making department.

So effort #1 looks like this. Chat, chat, chat. Weather, baseball, movies, TV, family, pets, news, neighbors, constructions, cars, stock market, etc., until something like, "I did the Avatar Course last year. It's a nine-day course about learning to live deliberately."

Congratulations. You just produced your first sub-product.

Effort #2 Planting Seeds of Interest

What is Avatar about? What do people get out of it? Why do people do it?

These are questions that people may or may not ask, but who doesn't like good news? A complimentary *Avatar Journal* is an example of an effort #2. Reading aloud from *Messages from the Heart* is an example of an effort #2. Reading aloud Chapter 6 of *Living Deliberately* is an example of an effort #2. The excitement in your eyes when you talk about Avatar is an example of an effort #2.

Successful Masters create excitement about Avatar by making friends and communicating their honest experiences from using and teaching Avatar. Their enthusiasm creates a wave of interest.

Avatar. Some things are better than you expect.

(For a detailed discussion of efforts #1 and #2, see Chapter 7, "Contact and Connection")

Effort #3: Describing Personal Benefits

Only rarely do you run into someone who is interested in Avatar because of the humanitarian work it is doing or the progress that it is making in creating a more peaceful world.

More usual is the person who is consciously or unconsciously asking, "What's in it for me?" They want to know how they will benefit from doing Avatar.

Here are some general benefits to get you started on your own list.

- You don't have to spend your whole life to achieve spiritual awareness.
- Thousands of people have confirmed that it works to remove emotional and mental barriers.
- Your thinking opens to new possibilities and new rewards.
- Discover how you can realize your dreams and life purposes.
- Get rid of the roadblocks and self-sabotaging beliefs that are causing you to fail.
- Take control of your own thinking and eliminate useless worries.
- Free attention that is trapped in the past.
- Access the life-shaping regions of your consciousness and take control.

- Know what you want and how to achieve it.
- Set your own standards for success and contentment.
- Reduce stress and become more alive and aware in every moment.
- Enjoy all aspects of your life.
- Heal long-term upsets and discover real compassion.
- Explore the deeper, spiritual issues of your life.
- Change how others perceive and relate to you.
- Experience the strength that comes from knowing the truth and achieving a metaphysical advantage.
- Accelerate your own self-evolvement with mystical, spiritual experiences.
- Enjoy the support of a worldwide network.
- Meet friends and soul-mates

Effort #4: Selling Books

Many Masters can move a person from a number one resource to a number five resource in the course of a single conversation or free lecture. This is your goal for talks and presentations to groups. At this stage the presentation should be more of an intellectual and entertaining program than an experiential event. Don't try to run them on experiential *ReSurfacing* exercises, but do discuss the effect of beliefs. Do belief exercises, goal-setting exercises and questions Q,R,& S of the Personality Profile. Don't try to immediately register the members of the local PTA, church group, study group, chess club for an Avatar Course, but **DO** set up an eye-popping book table with piles of *Living Deliberately*, *ReSurfacing*, Avatar audiotapes and *ReSurfacing Audio Workshop* tape sets. And always offer a free one-year's subscription to the *Avatar Journal* with any purchase. (Send their names and addresses to Star's Edge for the Journal subscriptions.)

You might be able to talk a person through these steps to the fifth completed sub-product level of "wants to experience an Avatar process" without selling them a book, but it is a big investment of time. It is exhausting and will actually reduce the number of Avatar students you will get.

Bottom line: you are much better off putting the same energy into selling as many books as you can and let the books work for you.

From a Master's Graduation Talk by Harry

I used to live on a farm in New York state. The previous owner of the farm had a large pond dug into the hillside, but the pond never filled up. It was really an acre-wide hole in the ground with a mud hole in the middle.

About a half mile away, sort of around the mountain, there was a spring. But the water from the spring ran down the wrong side of the mountain. I had a surveyor come and look over the situation. He told me the spring was 25 feet higher up the mountain than the bottom of my pond.

So I decided to bury a pipe from the spring to the pond. It was a big job. Rocks had to be moved, tree roots dug up, two thousand feet of pipe had to be placed so that it all flowed downhill. The ditch for the pipe had to be at least three feet deep to prevent freezing and had to drop an average of one foot per hundred feet of pipe. It was an enormous job. It took a lot of planning and a lot of effort. In the end it took over two years to complete.

Ah, but the satisfaction. When it was done, spring water was flowing into my pond at the rate of six gallons a minute. Okay, that isn't much into a pond that was designed for five million gallons, but this pipe flowed 24 hours a day. Six gallons a minute. Every minute! I could sleep late. I could read all day. It didn't matter. Six gallons a minute. People would walk up to me and ask, "What are you smiling about?" Six gallons a minute! Every minute. It didn't matter that it would take two more years for the pond to fill. The process was working for me. Time was on my side. (Smiling) You see it's still going on. Six gallons a minute. Even while I talk. It's a good feeling. Mostly we think about things that are running out. This is something that is running in. Six gallons a minute.

That is exactly what is starting every time you sell someone an Avatar book. You start Avatar running in. 🜲

(More details on how to sell books are discussed in Chapter 8.)

Effort #5: Follow-up, Inspire, and Involve

A follow-up letter or conversation is not a sales effort, it is an effort to inspire or involve. If it is your first follow-up after purchase, it is also a chance to say thanks.

Involvement, in this instance, means to inspire someone to think bigger, to decide with more certainty, or to act with more confidence. It is empowerment rather than entanglement. Whenever you ask a question that someone can answer and you really listen to their answer, you involve them. This is the purpose of your follow-up conversation. You invite the person to become source. "What did you think about (*Living Deliberately*, *ReSurfacing*, *Avatar Journal* or tape)?

Inspiring is awakening a viewpoint that realizes that something that seemed impossible can actually be done.—H

Accepting what they say, even if it is negative, is respecting their right to think and decide. If they ask personal case questions or abstract questions, answer them by asking, "What do you think (or believe)?" You act as a reminder of the relation between belief and experience. They have to become the expert on their own life. You don't want that post.

Effort #5, properly done, moves a person from theorizing, fantasizing, and dreaming to actually wanting to experience.

Follow-up Questions:

Do you think what you experience is ever affected by what you believe? (As a suggestion, discuss the two paragraphs beginning on the bottom of p. 31 in *Living Deliberately*.)

Are there any areas in your life where you would like to be more successful? (As a suggestion, discuss the last paragraph on p. 91 of *Living Deliberately*.)

Have you considered what it would be like to do Avatar? (As a suggestion, discuss the second paragraph on p. 53 of *Living Deliberately*.)

Did you know there is an Avatar workbook called *ReSurfacing*?

Is there anyone you'd like to order a book for? I can send it directly to them.

The sub-product of effort #5 is that the person expresses an interest in experiencing Avatar, no matter how vague or seemingly impossible.

Sometimes a follow-up conversation or correspondence will reveal that the person is already a step 5, step 6, or even step 7 sub-product.

Once you determine the level, you adopt the appropriate effort to keep them progressing.

Everyone You Meet Knows Someone

If you just keep this in mind, you will never run out of people to contact.

Once your relationship with a prospect has evolved to a telephone conversation, ask the person if they have ever done any formal self-exploration work. If not, did they ever discuss consciousness with anybody? Have they been involved with anything to do with consciousness? Yes? Who with? Do you think any of those people might be interested in receiving a free *Avatar Journal*? Get the names and, if available, addresses and telephone numbers. Otherwise, get a general location for the person and rely on the telephone book to supply an address.

Effort #6: Participatory Involvement

A step #6 resource wants to do Avatar, but they also want to go skiing, they want to visit China, they want to buy a motorcycle. Wanting stuff is familiar to them. They always want something. They are indoctrinated to want, but they have trouble achieving their wants. Your job at this stage is to motivate them to experience their dreams. To experientially explore. To pass from the vicarious world of TV and daydreaming into really being alive.

They have to take the step from imagining to experiencing. You invite them to an event or to a free private session.

One of the most deep-seated secondaries is deservability. Do they deserve Avatar? Do they deserve an investment of time and money in

There is a difference between knowing intellectually and experiencing.
—*Living Deliberately*

The best way to describe the flavor of wild strawberries is to show someone where they are found.
—H

themselves? They need a reason. And the best reason is to become more alive and more able.

Reasons for Finding out More about Avatar:

- You'll love it. It's right for you. You'll thank yourself in the future.

- It presents essential information on how to manage consciousness in a realistic and technically precise way. It is an exciting adventure.

- This is a valuable technology. There is nothing else like it. It handles self-sabotaging beliefs and behaviors that are costing you plenty.

- It sets the model for sanity, compassion, and companionship.

- It's a way of investing some of your time that has long-range benefits.

- It's touching something deeper than what is found in a rapidly changing society.

- We are all travelers entrusted with a fragment of the evolutionary map.

- It's the best investment you will ever make in yourself.

- Consciousness responds in certain ways. It has a nature. If you understand this nature, you can turn it to your advantage. If you don't understand the nature of consciousness, probably someone else is turning your consciousness to their advantage.

- Work on yourself requires diligence and effort. Wouldn't it be nice to have the best, most efficient tools available?

- Finding out about Avatar is something that will have an impact on the rest of your life.

- This is the time to work on yourself.

- Don't let the momentum of your life turn into boredom. If you need to make a mid-course correction, Avatar can help you through it.

- It's cheaper and more fun than a cruise vacation, a week at the shore, or a ski trip, and it leaves you with a foundation that you will use for the rest of your life.

- The major things that are keeping you from greater success are the unknowns in your own mind.

Shift their attention from their secondaries to the potential excitement and discoveries of participating in your event. You are bringing them alive.

Effort #6 events are more experiential than intellectual. They are more workshop oriented than seminar oriented. They look more like enthusiastic coaching, empowerment, and inspiration than like selling. (Chapter 11 discusses creating experiential events.)

The event is a time of safe vulnerability. It's a time of realization. The definition the person has been being clears up enough to let the definer shine through. One Master said, "It is the moment they realize we're not pretending."

Something that was abstract becomes real. Their Feel-Its turn on a little. Old discouragements start to resolve and new hope is born. It is an extraordinary moment.

The effort #6 event is also a time to introduce (privately or in a group) some of the expected results from acquiring and using the Avatar tools.

- Learn how to manage your beliefs.

- Learn how to take control of your life.

- Learn to better understand yourself.

- Learn to free yourself of self-sabotaging behaviors.

- Learn to see others as they truly are.

- Learn to achieve a meditative mind state and peak experiences at will.

- Learn to stay calm even while others are losing their cool.

- Learn how to magnetize your mind to attract what you desire.

- Learn how to recognize and resolve self-doubts.

- Learn how to pull your own strings and run your own life.

- Learn to live deliberately, proudly, and boldly.

The sub-product you are after is a commitment to a doable plan to do Avatar. The plan may include how to obtain finances, organize responsibilities, find a babysitter or a kennel, get time off. You keep their attention on the goal until the plan is complete, and they arrive and register.

It is a good idea to get a course deposit.

If you are working with a group, have them use their goal to do Avatar and complete the Life Alignment Program (Exercise 28 from *ReSurfacing*). From that they can create a plan.

Effort #7: Creating an Exciting Avatar Delivery

The decision to do Avatar is a turning point in a person's life. As with any turning point, the traveler is most comfortable when they can see the path ahead. This means that you must create and communicate a clear agenda for the course. It requires investigation of potential delivery sites, negotiation, and budget planning.

Usually agendas are printed and mailed several weeks in advance of the delivery. It's a good idea to have an agenda to hand out at effort #6.

The agenda takes an Avatar delivery from the level of abstraction to a concrete reality. It creates positive expectations for the experience. What is the theme of the delivery? Where is the delivery being held? Why is this location attractive? How does the student get there? Where does the student go when they get there? What is the lodging like? What does it cost? What is the restaurant situation?

Okay, on to the course. Where is registration being held? What is the course environment like? What is the exercise environment like? Couches? Hammocks? Are there trees? Mountains? Water? Historic buildings? Museums? Fabulous sunsets? Spiritual vibrations? What is the daily schedule?

Now, the extras. Walking tour of the city? Afternoon at the beach? Picnic in the forest? Catered lunch? Wednesday night Thoughtstorm? Friday night presentation by the local yoga teacher, natural food store owner, or Internet provider? (Request a talk that is more informative than a mere sales pitch—and, of course you will ask for a reciprocal invitation to present a talk to their group.)

You don't want to fill every minute with your agenda, because your students will need some quality alone time as well. One or two extras is quite sufficient.

This agenda serves two purposes. First it makes your Avatar deliveries real and attractive to your students. Second, because you mail it to everyone on your mailing list, it makes your Avatar deliveries real and attractive to future students.

See you at registration! (Reference: Chapter 12 "Signing Up Avatar Students")

Effort #8: Delivering Avatar

The quality of your Avatar delivery is determined by your ability to organize, to run positive control, and to spot and clear up student confusions by reference to the material they are studying. (Referencing your own experience or upper sections of the Avatar materials only adds confusion.)

The techniques and procedures for delivering Avatar are covered in your Master Course materials. They should be reviewed before each delivery.

Be certain that your Serious Drill is dispelling seriousness rather than causing humiliation. Don't rush the student or feed them your realizations. Stay compassionate. Remain attentive, but stay undefined. Stay out of your story.

Throughout the course there should be a gradual shifting of the student's attention from the Master to an understanding and appreciation of the materials, to a firsthand experience of a self that is independent of the phenomena of consciousness. The smoother this transition, the better the course.

Your deliveries can always be made a bit better or a bit worse. If you are always making them better, you will find that the amount of money and effort you need to expend in promoting your next delivery will diminish. Of course, the opposite is true as well.

Effort #9: Contributing to an Enlightened Planetary Civilization

For most students, somewhere near the end of the Avatar Course, there is a natural awakening of compassion for the world. Old animosities are replaced by a sincere desire that both friends and enemies awaken to the experience of Avatar. This is a good time for you to ask for prospects for Avatar. Collect the names and interests of ex-lovers, ex-spouses, ex-partners, ex-associates, as well as current associates and friends. (If you recommend the Avatar graduate for the Master Course, he or she may want to partner with you to deliver to current associates and friends, but the ex-people are probably yours alone.)

Chapter 7

Contact and Connection

Resource	Effort	Sub-Product
1. A person who has never heard of Avatar.	First contact	A person who knows that Avatar is a course about learning to live deliberately.
2. A person who has heard of Avatar (good or bad).	Expose them to the actual testimonials of people who have completed Avatar.	A person who knows that people have benefited greatly from Avatar.

The Tools Of Diplomacy

Contact and connection are the fundamental skills for establishing interactions with others. They are the tools of the ambassador. It doesn't matter if you come from across the hall or from an extraterrestrial civilization. They are, in fact, so fundamental as a purpose among living creatures that there is a general assumption that everyone knows how to contact and connect. Nothing could be further from the truth.

Contacting someone means attracting enough of their attention to support a meaningful exchange of communication. Establishing contact is an outflow of effort. It is usually done face to face or via mail or e-mail, telephone, or some other form of data transmission. This is the time when you announce yourself (establish your presence as a communication terminal) and learn the other person's name.

Connecting with someone means to temporarily share their viewpoint. Connecting is an inflow of the other person's viewpoint. It requires that you suspend judgment and listen with neutral attention. It means knowing and respecting the customs, manners, and social rituals that open the path to communication beyond superficial expression.

Providing that the person you contact is not overwhelmed or otherwise involved in something and puts suspicion aside, your effort to contact and connect is secretly welcomed and even considered flattering. Repeated contacts convey a sense of importance to the person.

Establishing a Contact Leading to a Connection

There are many ways of attracting attention (clowning, exhibition, bragging, acting rudely, threatening, attacking), but the attention attracted probably won't support meaningful communication sufficient to avoid hostility and lead to connection.

Until contact and connection are established, an Avatar Master's role is that of ambassador.

Depending upon the means you employ, a contact leading to a connection can be achieved by:

1. clever advertising

2. by a formal or informal introduction and referral

3. by physical proximity for an extended period

4. by alignment of attention

5. by shared aesthetic appreciation

In dealing with persons as intractable and as difficult to influence as a pig or a fish, the whole secret of success depends on finding the right way of approach. One must first rid oneself of all prejudice and, so to speak, let the psyche of the other person act on one without restraint.
—I Ching

6. by shared agreements

7. by surprise (pleasant)

Each of these is discussed below.

1. Clever Advertising

Here's a quick summary of how to design successful ads. It's called the ACIDA formula.

gain	**Attention**
spark	**Curiosity**
develop	**Interest**
generate	**Desire**
initiate	**Action**

The opening sentence of your letter, or headline of your ad, or banner of your Avatar delivery announcement should capture the prospect's attention. If it doesn't, the ad is a waste of time and money. This is an aspect of your advertising that should be given considerable thought and planning. What type of person do you want to reach? What attracts their attention? What benefits are they looking for? This is a good opportunity for a Thoughtstorm session and continuous testing. When your headline is so good that people stop what they are doing to read or listen, you're there.

Curiosity is sparked by mystery. Often it is generated visually by photos or illustrations. What is under the box? Behind the door? Why? What does it mean? It's an intensification of attention.

Interest is a sustained flow of attention. Once you have gained attention and sparked curiosity, you must offer <u>easily understandable, fascinating,</u>

valuable information. Score your written copy against these three qualities. A slight change in wording can make a big difference in how much interest you develop. Interest is developed in direct ratio to the ease with which the reader (or listener, or viewer) can give answers to the question, "Why do I want to know about this?" If the answers are not obvious, you can provide a few.

Desire is generated by aligning the benefits of your offer (a book, tape, workshop) with the promise of achieving a goal or fulfilling a need that the person frequently has attention on. What are the goals or needs of the type of person you are addressing? Is your statement of benefits a satisfactory answer to their question, "What's in it for me?" If it is, you will generate desire. The primary that you're working them toward is, "This is just what I need."

The same action may be considered difficult or easy, depending upon how it is presented. The easier you make it for the customer to respond to what you are offering, the more action you will initiate. Add fun, bonus offers, and special events, and you'll initiate even more action. Make sure your ad tells the person exactly what to do (prominently) and encourages that they act promptly.

2. Introductions and Referrals

As a general benefit to the planet, establish a habit of introducing people to each other. It is a three-step process: 1) mention names, 2) mention your relationship with the person being introduced, and 3) offer an opening topic of conversation. Even if they never do Avatar, the introductions assist the integration of belief systems.

Examples:

> "Hi Jan, I'd like you to meet Jim. He handles our advertising at Star's Edge. He's good at marketing."

> "Mary, this is Bob. He works at the hospital. He just finished Avatar."

> "Ralph, this is Susan. She's an old friend. She owns a great cat."

If you have set the example often enough, people will introduce you to their friends and acquaintances. This is contact-made-easy. You are ready to begin connecting.

Most of the time, you are going to have to fly solo and make your own introduction. Maybe it's someone you meet in a waiting line or at a party. Maybe it's a referral from a book buyer, an Avatar or another Master. Maybe it's face to face, or by telephone or mail. In any case, you should say your name and a compliment (or what you do or who you know), followed by a simple question.

> "Hi, my name is Harry. I'm an Avatar trainer. What do you do?"

> "Hi, my name is Harry. I'm a friend of Jennifer's. I love your smile."

For ex-people referrals,

> "Hi, my name is Harry. Your name came up when I was reminiscing with Jack Small. Do you remember him?"

Make an effort to meet people who have already invested time and money in self-discovery books and courses. How did they find out about the courses they took? (This is valuable information.) What made them decide to take it? (This is a gold mine of information.) What did they like best? Was it worth it? Would they do it again? Listen to their wins and disappointments.

Remember, as long as a person is not overwhelmed or otherwise involved in something, your effort to contact and connect is welcome. It doesn't matter if you stammer a little or have trouble thinking of something to say. Your attention is flattering.

A friendly smile to the world at large makes quiet moments comfortable.

If you ever do run into a hostile reaction, just realize it's their creation. *"Observe, these are hostile people. Their role in life is to be hostile. That is what they do. Don't take it personally."*

3. Physical Proximity

Physical proximity with others happens on airplanes, in airports, on trains, in grocery checkout lines, in any situation that involves waiting. Why not screw up your courage and turn the waiting into an opportunity to establish contact with another individual? Even if you don't end up with a prospect, you will be surprised by what you might learn, e.g., "Oh, there's a support group that meets on Friday evenings at our church to discuss things like that." (Path of opportunity?)

4. Alignment of Attention

Notice what a person's attention is on. Establish contact with the person by commenting on the subject that the person is looking at, e.g., "Have you ever seen so many people?" (If their attention is on the people, they will respond.) "Oh, by the way, my name is Harry." (Listen and repeat their name aloud for confirmation.)

Under alignment of attention come social clubs and groups. You should belong to several. There are bridge circles, golf buddies, history buffs, computer clubs, singles bars, special interest groups (SIGs) of every variety.

5. Shared Aesthetic Appreciation

There is something about the experience of beauty that opens people up. It may be a natural beauty like a sunset or spectacular view, creations such as dance, figure skating, or drama. Between acts at a theater is a great time to make contacts. Art displays and beautiful architecture or a moving piece of music make people want to connect. Making an effort to attend such events not only offers the opportunity to establish many contacts, but it also nourishes your soul.

Combination coffee shops and bookstores are becoming increasingly popular. People want to make connections and socialize, but they're afraid. You make it easy by taking the first step.

6. Shared Agreements

People are naturally attracted to others who share and support their viewpoints. (The classic: "I think that everyone here can agree that we're here.")

7. By Surprise (Pleasant)

People like to be pleasantly surprised by special validation or extra attention. As long as it is perceived as sincere (there is a lot of suspicion in the collective consciousness), it offers a great opportunity to establish contact and connection.

The Last Word on Contact

Establishing contact is an outflow of effort. It requires boldness and initiative. Usually the more boldness and initiative, the more successful the contacts. For example, it requires more boldness and initiative to walk up and introduce yourself to someone or to deliver a talk in front of a group than it does to put up a poster or mail out a flyer. Somewhere in between is making telephone calls.

Self-consciousness and fear of rejection are deeply and often painfully indoctrinated in some minds. Embarrassment and the possibility of humiliation encourage separation and solitude, but in the business of creating an enlightened planetary civilization, they lead to failure. Boldness and initiative are not inborn qualities. They are skills developed from practice. Acquired abilities. (See Chapter 4, "Building Skills")

The most frequent cause of failing to create large deliveries is a hesitation to make contact with lots of potential customers. Successful Masters think in terms of hundreds of contacts and connections for each registered student. It really is a matter of numbers. When your skill at contact and connection improve, the ratio of contacts to students goes down.

The best advice regarding contact and connection is always GO FOR IT! Be bold. Any temporary pain of embarrassment (and there may be none) cannot begin to compare to the regret for a life of missed opportunities. Don't hang back. Step up; make contacts and connections. You're not taking a survey on what people think of you. You're on a mission to create an enlightened planetary civilization. Live boldly.

If you have trouble establishing contact with twenty to fifty people per day, do The Professional Course (Master Course B). The Professional Course addresses the subject of presence and embarrassment at a deep level of creation. It is recommended for every Master.

In the meantime, if you have difficulty moving out of your social comfort zone, work with the following primaries:

I am happy to be me.

People like me.

I am not afraid to initiate contact with people.

Connection is a Time for Qualifying

Qualifying is determining whether or not a person wants to improve some aspect of his or her life and is willing and able to invest the time, money, and effort necessary to do it.

Probably every person could benefit from Avatar, but not every person is ready for Avatar. This is a step where you, as a Master, determine whether or not you will even bring up the subject of Avatar. Let's be realistic. There are a finite number of people you can introduce to Avatar in your lifetime. Is this going to be one of them? They don't have to be. Maybe your time would be better spent on your next contact.

Done objectively, qualifying is an act of discernment rather than judgment. Until you learn to do it well, you can expect to waste a lot of time.

Qualifying is done by listening, observing, or questioning. Have they ever been involved in a spiritual practice? Do they wonder about the meaning of life? What is most important to them? What are their goals? Are they interested in self-improvement? Do they have a willingness to look beyond their current assumptions and beliefs? Are they real? Are they searching? Are they reaching? These are questions that you keep in mind but do not necessarily ask. Just listen and you will learn the answers without asking.

This is the time for exchanging pleasantries about life or work. Describe yourself as an Avatar

Master, but don't start talking about Avatar. Not yet. Leave it at, "It's a course about exploring human potential." Your reluctance to discuss it any further will spark curiosity in the qualified prospect. Steer the conversation in a different direction. Have they ever practiced meditation? Was it worth it? Did they like it? What did they hope to accomplish? Your interest is in learning about them. Are they currently involved in a spiritual practice? Is it hard? Are they making progress? If they don't eventually steer the conversation back to Avatar or human potential, they're probably not a prospect. If they do steer it back, ask a question to find out how interested they really are. Do you think a person can modify his or her own behavior to be happier or more successful? What if I told you there is a set of tools that will allow you to re-engineer your own consciousness. Would you be interested?

Yes?

Then you say, "Let me recommend a book to you, *Living Deliberately*. Period. Further questions? Nicely say, "It's in the book. Would you like me to get you a copy?" That is how really productive Masters handle inquiries about Avatar. They never launch into long explanations or monopolize the conversation with their sales pitch. And they never deliver a lecture, unless that's why the people are there. They create connection and curiosity, and let the book create the interest.

Three Categories

As a rule of thumb, your random contacts will fall into three categories.

You will find that about a third of the people you meet have a self-deservability issue. These people will not let themselves have Avatar no matter how available you make it. They are not interested in knowing themselves better. They are actually seeking less awareness of self rather than more. The subject of self depresses them. They would rather blame someone or something else for their problems. If you offer Avatar to them, they feel compelled to ridicule it. They will steer any discussion of Avatar toward a "prove it" argument. So, unless you enjoy feeling defensive, don't waste your time.

Another third of the people you meet will express an interest in Avatar, but their interest is really a dangling bait to get your attention. They are clearly not prepared spiritually or emotionally or financially to do Avatar. Everything looks pretty much the same from their viewpoint. Often they are committed to some answer that they would like to sell you. Here is where you find the get-rich-quick schemers who invite you to talk about Avatar only until they can steer the conversation to the wonders of their synthetic-natural food supplement weight-loss program.

The best you can do with this group is to offer them a book (*Living Deliberately*) in exchange for a sample of their product or their book. You never know. Some become very good Masters.

The last third of the people you meet are interested in improving themselves. They are seekers. Recent surveys show that over 30 percent of the people interviewed were more interested in achieving enlightenment than in achieving material success. (Wow, huh?) Some of these view self-development as a means to an end, and some of them view self-development as the end. Many have been disappointed by former practices, but much to their credit, they are still searching for truth. This sometimes makes them a bit hostile when you first approach them.

Overall, they are responsible and look to their own thoughts and actions to correct life's problems—sometimes too much so. They are vulnerable to guilt feelings, but they are also capable of powerful charitable acts. These are the people you want to invest time in. Provide them with a small amount of relevant information about Avatar, and they will have little difficulty finding the money and time to buy and read a book.

Chapter 8

Presentations

Resource	Effort	Sub-Product
3. A person who has heard something favorable about Avatar.	Align the benefits of Avatar with a personal need, a goal, or with resolving a personal situation.	A person who has a hunch that Avatar might offer some personal benefits and is seeking more information.

Events and Presentations are not the Same

A typical Avatar delivery has been preceded by at least seven presentations and three events.

Presentations and events should not be confused. A presentation is for people who do not own a book about Avatar. Its goal is to rekindle an individual's hopes and dreams. Its sub-products are 1) a person who knows that Avatar is a course about living deliberately, 2) a person who knows that people have benefited greatly from Avatar, 3) a person who has a hunch that Avatar might offer some personal benefits, and 4) the sale of a book or tape about Avatar.

Examples of presentations are personal discussions with interested individuals, free lectures, talks to groups, mini-seminars at expos and fairs, and proposals to teachers and businessmen. Presentations rarely run over thirty minutes.

Presentations:

Materials required
>
> flip chart
>
> marker
>
> book table
>
> a supply of books and *Avatar Journals*
>
> invoices
>
> 3 x 5 cards for names and addresses

Three Steps: Foundation, Context, Questions

The overall purpose of your presentation is to persuade a person to find out more about Avatar. This means that you are going to leave the person with some haunting questions. Yes, that's right. Your presentation is most successful when it stimulates questions and is least successful when it presents answers.

Your first job is to create the foundation and context for the listener's questions.

Step 1. Foundation Guidelines

1. *"In 1987, an educational psychologist named Harry Palmer outlined an intriguing series of mental procedures that could be easily taught to just about anybody. The amazing thing about these procedures is that when they are done in a certain order, they become a combination that unlocks the secrets of human consciousness."*

2. *"Why do you think someone would want to unlock the secrets of human consciousness?"* (This is not a rhetorical question; you want answers. If you're addressing a group, you make a list of the answers on a flip chart, black board or white board. Coax

with *"Why?"* Let the individual or group run out of answers. Use your own judgment as to whether or not you add any of your own answers to their answers.)

3. *"Avatar is a nine-day course that teaches you how to discover the combination to your own life."*

"Does it work? That is the question. Only you can answer it."

"The course has been translated into 14 languages and has spread to 58 countries. Since 1987, almost 50,000 people have paid $2000 each to go through the Avatar Course. And guess what? If anybody wasn't satisfied, their money was refunded. How many refunds were there in 50,000 people? Less than 100! Only one person in 500 asked for their money back."

"How about the other 499 people? They had experiences like these:"

(Read short excerpts from several success stories.)

Step 2. Context

1. *"Have you ever heard the expression, Seeing is believing? What does that mean?"* (Get answers.)

2. *"What if, as some have suggested, it is the other way around, Believing is seeing?"*

3. *"How do you believe something?"* (Get an answer. Ask, *"How exactly do you do that?"* Get another answer. Ask, *"How exactly do you do that?"*) Leave this step with a general agreement: *"How a person believes is one of the mysteries of consciousness. (Point to the list.) Do you agree?"*

Step 3. Questions

This presentation can be modified into a book sales patter.

1. *"Let's play what-if for a minute. What if Avatar unlocked the mystery of how to believe something into existence? Just <u>what if</u>? Would that interest you? What would you believe about yourself into existence? What would you like to experience? Think about it for a minute. There are no right or wrong answers."*

"If you could create the reality that you prefer, what would you create?"

(After a pause.) *"If you would like to know more about the discovery and development of Avatar, I recommend this book, Living Deliberately."* (Hold up.)

"If you would like to sample some of the Avatar processes yourself to see if they work for you, I recommend this book, ReSurfacing." (Hold up.)

"We'll include a one-year's subscription to the Avatar Journal with either purchase." (Hold up.) *"Thank you very much. I'll be at the book table for anyone who has any questions."*

Quantity and Quality of Presentations Equal Students

Masters who make (or host) the most presentations have the largest Avatar deliveries. Seek every opportunity to present Avatar and sell Avatar books. Here's another sample presentation for clubs and study groups.

1. Opening Curtain

If you are planning to do an exercise from *ReSurfacing* (suggested choices: #6 "Controlling

Attention" or #17 "Compassion Exercise"), **open with it.** This has the effect of creating immediate involvement with the audience. If more than one Master is presenting, let one lead the exercise and then finish by introducing the speaker.

2. The Speaker's Introduction

If it's for you, write it yourself. Let someone else give it, but offer them something to say. Usually they are grateful and will read it word for word. Write something (but not everything) about your background and accomplishments that will interest the audience and give them the impression that you are a credible speaker on the subject being presented.

3. Orient the Audience with your Opening Lines

"What I want to talk to you about is committing some of your time and energy to learning more about yourself. I hope that's on your agenda for this lifetime— to learn more about yourself. I'm going to share some information with you and invite you to experience a couple of exercises that may give you greater insight.

"If I'm really good, you'll be on the Avatar Course tomorrow.

"If I'm not quite that good, maybe you'll at least leave with a book to read.

"And if I'm terrible, then at least you will go away with an experience to avoid in the future."

4. Tell the Audience How They Will Benefit from Learning about Themselves

"People who commit some of their time and energy to answering the big questions of life: Who am I? Why am I here? What do I want out of life? How much of my own destiny do I control? have a much better chance for success and happiness than people who live indoctrinated lives and are afraid to question their own assumptions.

"Life is an adventure. It requires an adventurous attitude. You probably wouldn't be here if you didn't have a least the glowing ember of an adventurous attitude.

"The best adventurers equip themselves for their expedition. You don't start out for the North Pole without some food supplies, a tent, and at least a can of Sterno. Now you might make it with that sort of equipment.

"And you might not.

"Your chances improve if your food is chosen for cold weather, your tent is insulated, and you carry a propane stove instead of a can of sterno. You see, the better your equipment, the more likely and the more comfortable your success.

"The same applies to tools. If you want to achieve something, say building a house, the better your tools, the easier and more likely you are to succeed.

"Now take these big questions: Who am I? Why am I here? What do I want out of life? Finding the answers to these questions involves an inner journey. A trip to your own pole.

"You're not going to let someone else tell you who you are.

"You're not going to let someone else tell you why you exist. Here, this is your purpose in life.

"Would you let someone tell you that?

"If you would, then your adventurous spirit is pretty weak.

"Would you let someone else tell you what you want?

"You would rebel. Maybe you'd even choose the opposite of what they said to demonstrate your independence. I've done that, haven't you? Done just the opposite of what someone told me to do—done just the opposite deliberately.

"But you know what? You don't want the opposite anymore that you wanted what they offered.

"Advice really isn't much good when it comes to answering the big questions. You have to make the inner journey and answer them yourself. It won't do you any good to imitate the answers that someone else found.

"You can read the great philosophers or religious men and accept their answers—but they aren't your answers. Did you ever try to wear someone else's shoes?

"You know, when we all look at the same thing, we each see it a little differently. That's because we are all looking from a different point of view—a different location in space, through different eyes. If you rely on what someone else saw, you are getting their point of view.

"It may be an agreeable point of view. It might be artful, or entertaining, or seem very wise, but it's not your point of view. In fact, when you accept their point of view, you don't exist any longer.

"How many people are here who don't exist?

"If you are living with someone else's viewpoint, you don't exist. If you are living with your parents' viewpoint or a teacher's viewpoint or a preacher's viewpoint—some viewpoint that you were persuaded to put on—you don't exist.

"Do you ever feel like you don't exist?

"One of the big discoveries that people make on Avatar is that I exist.

"Wow! There's something more here than a name and a mind full of information. I exist.

"As soon as you discover that I exist, you know that no one else can answer the big questions for you: Who am I? Why am I here? What do I want out of life?

"Do you want to know the answers to those questions? Then you have to make the inner journey. You have to travel across your own consciousness and find out what's at the pole. You have to go yourself. Either go, or settle for a life in which you don't exist.

"These are powerful ideas, aren't they?

"So we come to Avatar. Avatar is a set of tools. Very fine tools. Tested and proven tools that equip you for this inner journey to the pole of your consciousness. They are tools that will keep you comfortable on this journey. If you're not comfortable, what will happen? You'll give up. How many people have set out to answer these questions and given up? You give up and accept someone else's answer. You pretend to be someone else.

"That won't happen with Avatar, because the tools of Avatar make the journey fun. You're not going to have to meditate, or give up sex, (I saw some relief there), or pray every day.

"Avatar is effective. It doesn't need to set up any excuse that it can later fall back on to explain your failure. Oh, you didn't pray hard enough.

*"It's easier, faster, and more effective than anything else that has **ever** been available. That's a bold statement! But it is a true statement. Since 1987, thousands of students have successfully completed Avatar. "*

(Read one or two inspirational success stories.)

(If other Avatars or Masters are present: Some of them are here and will talk with you. Others send you open messages in the *Avatar Journal* and the *Messages from the Heart* press book.)

"The crux of their messages, repeated over and over, is use the tools and make the journey.

"Who am I? Why am I here? What do I want out of life? The answers to these questions are the most precious secrets of life. Nothing that you can ever do or own will give you the satisfaction that knowing these answers will give you. Nothing! These are the answers that Avatar equips you to find.

"Committing to this journey is the most important decision of your life. Who am I? Why am I here? What do I want out of life? You can experience the big answers first-hand, on your own journey, but you will never truly speak them. No one can. Isn't that interesting?

"Experiencing the real answers is worth more than having all the answers to any question the mind can raise.

"Experiencing the real answers to Who am I? Why am I here? What do I want out of life? is the difference between an indoctrinated person with a mental closet full of thoughts and an enlightened person.

"I know this may be a lot to digest. It's probably not what you expected, but that is the stopping power of truth. You deserve to know the truth.

"The Avatar Course contains a set of exercises that develop a set of skills. Easy to learn. And these skills are the exact combination that unlock the human mind.

"Once the mind is unlocked, there are rundowns that allow you to manage the contents of your mind. You will discover that the contents of your mind are determining your life, your success or failure, your attitude, your happiness—all of it preprogrammed by these contents that you could not before get to, could not change. Now you can. Avatar lets you start living your life deliberately.

"Is this is of interest to you?

"You can begin exploring the exercises next week in a ReSurfacing workshop. It is the first step of your adventure. One of the Avatar Masters here will be glad to give you more information and provide you with registration forms.

"They're not going to hard-sell you. If you're ready, you're ready. If you're not, you're not. Life will tell you when it's time to take this journey.

"There are also Avatar Journals, tapes, and books on the back table for sale. If you don't have any money but are still interested, leave us your name and we'll add you to our mailing list.

"There's one special at the book table that I particularly want to tell you about. It's called the Power

Package and consists of the book Living Deliberately,
which talks about the discovery and development of
Avatar, the ReSurfacing workbook that contains 30
exercises for exploring consciousness, a Ten Actions
Booklet that contains ten things you can do every day to
make your life better, a Create Magic In Your Life
audiotape and a one-year's subscription to the Avatar
Journal. If you bought these separately it would cost you
$55, but if you buy them as a package, your cost is $25.
This is a good investment in yourself."

(Taking questions from the audience can save or
destroy your presentation. It depends on how
skillfully and credibly you answer. If you
reactively assert importance or a superior attitude,
or go out of character, you can undermine
everything else that you have said. It's risky. The
safest and best course of action is to offer to meet
privately with anyone who has questions.)

5. a. The Big Finish

If your budget can possibly afford it, rent a large
screen TV and end your talk with the Avatar video.

"Here are some people talking about their Avatar
experiences. You will see that they are not paid actors or
famous sports figures. They were not compensated in
any way for their endorsements, and they didn't
rehearse or read from scripts. In other words, it's real.
See if you can feel what they are feeling."

<<Have video cued.>>

5. b. The No-TV, No-VCR Option (or the Not-Quite-So-Big Finish)

"Let me read you what someone wrote after doing Avatar:" (Read your favorite success story—BUT JUST ONE.)

6. After the Applause. (Yes, You Clap Too)

"Thank you. If any of you have questions, I'll be available back by the book table to answer them."

(All of the above can be adapted for a one-on-one presentation.)

A Lecture/Workshop Created By Wizards

At the 1997 Wizard Course, students participated in outlining a 30-minute talk on Avatar that would inform and result in the sale of a book or a person's registering for the ReSurfacing Workshop. This is an interesting lecture/workshop in that it bridges the gap between a presentation and an event.

Materials required for this event:

- overhead projector
- screen
- transparencies
- extension cord
- table for projector
- flip chart with easel
- markers for chart

Also large supplies of the following:

- folded business card containing the
- Compassion Exercise
- *Living Deliberately* books
- *ReSurfacing* books
- *ReSurfacing* audiotapes
- *Avatar Journals*
- registration forms

1. (For an informal presentation) Invite people for a chat about Avatar. (For a more formal presentation) Present a free lecture on How to Create What You Want in Life. (For an invitation to address a group) Offer a talk on the Basic Principle of Avatar. Experiment with the best times for the event (morning, afternoon, evening) and locations (hotel, home, library, church, school) for your area.

Call your Avatar graduates and find out if they have a friend they would like to interest in Avatar. Call your friends. Put announcements in the local newspaper, flyers at the health food store, posters at libraries and churches. This is the effort you exchange for students. Keep calling, keep talking, keep inviting. Build group excitement with other Masters.

2. Night of the event. Introduce yourself briefly and say: *"Let's start with an exercise from the ReSurfacing book. The objective of the exercise is to convey an experience of the expansion and integration that is opened by the Avatar materials. It's a beautiful way for us to begin."* Do the Expansion Exercise, bottom of page 90 in *ReSurfacing*.

3. When everyone is comfortably back from the Expansion Exercise, ask the following rhetorical questions to create nods of agreement with the group:

"Do you ever feel like you make the same mistakes again and again?"

"Do you ever feel like there is more to your life than you are actually experiencing?"

"Do you ever feel like there is a solution that you can't quite remember?"

Open the flip chart to a page with the following question written at the top. *"What is keeping us from fully experiencing our dreams?"*

Invite people to call out answers. Write the answers that are called out as situations. Someone calls out "fear." Write "because I am afraid." Someone calls out "money." Write "because of money."

After you have a whole list of beliefs and limiting situations written down, say, *"I want to read you something from Harry Palmer that I highlighted in the book Living Deliberately: The Discovery and Development of Avatar."* Read aloud from page 31 where you previously highlighted.

"I started counseling people with problems and learned to observe and listen closely. Mental patterns began to appear. Little by little I developed a technique...When the technique worked, it unraveled and opened to a profound concept: I create my experiences according to what I believe. What a peculiar notion! Until now it seemed everyone assumed that people created their beliefs according to what they had experienced. What if it was the other way around?"

Ask rhetorically, *"What if it is the other way around?"* Go through the situations on the flip chart. *"Are you creating these situations by what you believe? (Dramatically) Are your beliefs keeping you from experiencing your dreams?"* When you have everyone's agreement that this might be so, read aloud the three paragraphs on transparent beliefs from page 81 in *ReSurfacing*. *"A belief is...(continue to)...degree of vulnerability."*

An overhead projector is used to show how beliefs can shadow someone's dream. Start with a transparency showing illustrations of people doing their dreams, e.g., traveling, buying a house, getting married. Have several previously prepared transparencies: 1) someone hurrying and looking at her watch; have it labeled NO TIME, 2) someone with their pockets empty and bills all around them; have it labeled NO MONEY, 3) someone looking confused and apathetic; have it labeled NO PLAN.

Start the group looking at the dream and place the NO TIME transparency over the dream. *"What happens? The dream isn't quite so clear."* Place the NO MONEY transparency over the dream. *"The dream is less clear."* Dramatically ask, *"What is the final dream killer?"* Silently place the NO PLAN transparency over the rest.

Refer back to the situations on the flip chart. *"Any one of these can create a reality that obscures your dream. And guess what?"* Hold up one of the transparencies and look through it. *"Yes, they're transparent beliefs."*

"Wouldn't you rather create the reality you prefer?" Remove all the transparencies back to the dream, and then cover the dream again with the transparencies. Let the audience think.

4. *"Creating the reality that you prefer is exactly what the Avatar Course is about. It's a course about how to change the transparent beliefs that have been obstructing you into beliefs that can assist you. So at least now you can get rid of this one."* Remove the transparency labeled NO PLAN.

5. Have a supply of the Compassion Exercise/business cards with your name, address, and telephone number. Give each person a card and go over the instructions with the group. Have them think of someone they have an upset with.

Give them time. When they have selected a person, read each of the steps and wait for them to do it.

6. After *"Just like me, this person is learning about life,"* pause for a bit. Then in conclusion say, *"If you still want to learn more about life, there are copies of **Living Deliberately** and **ReSurfacing** for sale at the book table and I (or one of the other Avatar Masters here) will be glad to take your registration for one of the ReSurfacing workshops that are scheduled in this area. Thank you."*

The above should all be rehearsed (e.g., at a Masters' weekend) until it can be done smoothly and professionally. Feel free to modify anything you don't like. The success variables of the event are a) time and place of the event, b) qualification of people attending, c) presence, appearance and professionalism of the speaker, e.g., a Professional Course graduate, d) care, presence and appearance of supporting Masters.

Public Relations Emergency

There is one more type of presentation you should know about. It occurs when a hungry-for-a-story reporter corners you to ask about some lurid rumor or potentially embarrassing situation, e.g., "Wasn't so-and-so who robbed a bank, committed suicide, stole the handicapped children's' toys, your Avatar student?"

First, decide if you want to comment at all. Remember, reporters are not above embarrassing you, flattering you, or threatening you to get information. If you do not have the support and cooperation of a group, don't assume the role of spokesperson for the group. If you don't have the resources to establish the actual facts, don't assume the role of expert. "No comment."

However, if you are the appointed spokesperson or the local expert, rather than responding willy-nilly to a reporter's sudden interest or pressure, you should make a presentation.

Since you are going to need time to prepare your presentation, memorize and use this exactly worded statement to allow you time to find the facts.

I AM AWARE THAT THERE ARE SOME REPORTS. I AM CURRENTLY GATHERING DETAILS. AS SOON AS I AM SURE OF THE FACTS, I WILL ANNOUNCE A BRIEFING. WOULD YOU LIKE TO BE CALLED?

That buys you time to find out the following:

1. Does Star's Edge know there is a potential public relations emergency?

2. What caused the situation? What could have prevented the situation?

3. How many people have been directly affected?

4. What is the likely outcome? When will you know more?

5. Is there any ongoing risk?

6. What are the major concerns at the present time? What is being done to achieve (or resolve) them?

Create a concise written statement that rephrases the above questions into answers. (e.g., *The situation was the result of some personal motives that we are not aware of. I don't know what might have prevented it. Unfortunately, both families have been affected. We are cooperating with the authorities. The results of their investigation should be known soon. There is no reason for people to worry. We are increasing our efforts to screen inappropriate clients with preregistration interviews.*)

Answer factually without speculation, opinion, marketing, or propaganda attack. Hand your statement to reporters before your briefing.

At your press briefing, read the statement **EXACTLY** as you have written it. A favorite ploy of reporters is to get you to contradict your own statement. Don't, because if you do, the contradiction will almost certainly become the focus of their story.

If they ask for something that wasn't in the statement and that you are unsure of, answer, *"I don't have that information."* If they ask for an opinion, answer, *"I'd rather not give an opinion."* If they ask for speculation, answer, *"I'd rather not speculate."*

Don't respond too quickly to questions. If there is good news, tone it down and make it guarded. Get off a question that you have responded to by asking, *"Are there any other questions?"* If a reporter persists in digging into something you've already responded to, answer, *"I've already responded to that."* If they ask what your response was, answer, *"Read your notes."*

Practice. Be concise and brief. Do not fall victim to attention or applause. Keep your identity, ego, and personality out of this presentation.

Chapter 9

Selling Books

Resource	Effort	Sub-Product
4. A person who has some interest in Avatar.	Sell them an Avatar book or tape and/or get their name and address for an *Avatar Journal.*	A person who possesses accurate information about Avatar. Someone who has tested it out mentally.

One of the biggest and goofiest mistakes that new Masters make is to contact someone whom they've never met and who has never heard of Avatar and try to sell them a two-thousand dollar course. Hello?

It is hoped that after reading Chapter 6, they will realize this is a little bit like trying to enter the Empire State building on the twenty-fifth floor.

The first major hurdle to getting a person to take the Avatar Course is getting a book into their hands and getting them to read it. Even if someone else is paying for their course, which is seldom a good idea, this step should not be left out.

There are two approaches to selling Avatar books: marketing and sales. These two subjects are often grouped into one category, but they are not always the same.

Marketing

Marketing uses advertising to create a desire for a book by exciting copy, charts, illustrations, and pictures. The desire created is usually to be more like someone the person admires and/or less like someone the person resists, e.g., "Avatars are the most aware and compassionate group of people in the world. Avatars don't sabotage their own efforts with defeating beliefs."

Favorite desires are to be seekers, explorers, discoverers, enlightened beings, independent, discerning, wise, awake, really alive. The fundamental message is that if you want to start manifesting these qualities in your life, buy and read *Living Deliberately*.

Running ads, handing out flyers, writing letters, mailing book offers, putting up posters and generally broadcasting to people good reasons for buying the book are marketing actions. (Reference: "Clever Advertising" in Chapter 7.)

Sales

Selling is the final effort of marketing. In its simplest form, it is writing a receipt and filling an order. Beyond that, it becomes helping a qualified prospect find personal good reasons to purchase a book.

Remember, promoting yourself or your product is marketing. Listening and observing and offering a reason to buy is sales.

Sales begins with an investigation of your potential customer. This is done with Feel-Its, observation, a body language signal that you are sincerely interested, and questioning that reveals a difficulty that your customer has attention stuck on.

A wise Master knows that a difficulty is really an obstacle to some goal. Sometimes it takes some extrapolation to discover the goal behind the difficulty. But you can always tell when you're moving in the right direction, because the person's interest will suddenly come alive. Even if you don't manage to sell the person a book, you have benefited the person by shifting his or her attention from obstacles to goals.

The second step of sales is aligning one of the expected results from reading *Living Deliberately* or *ReSurfacing* with the person's obstructed goal. (See effort #3 for a list of benefits.)

If the person has an objection to buying and reading the book, just ask them what would make them change their mind.

Master Anecdote: Book Table Selling

People tend to talk about money in superficial ways, so I just eliminate that with my question. "Aside from not having enough money, what gives you the most difficulty in life?" I get a lot of social answers and pretense, but the kernel of truth in their answer always boils down to not having enough control of (or over) something or someone.

So I say, "Most people don't know how to use the power of their consciousness to (determine, control, affect) whatever their control issue is." This statement almost always meets with agreement.

Then I say, "If I could recommend a book to you that would show you how to use the power of your consciousness, would you buy it?"

This usually gets a noncommittal answer. "Maybe."

And I hold ReSurfacing up, but I always hold it upside down. They usually turn their head trying to read it, and we clown around for a minute about the book being upside down. "Upside down, you'd ReSurface in China." That lightens them up and they buy the book.

Master Anecdote: Story into Book Selling

When someone asks me about Avatar, I tell them the story of how Harry became frustrated with all the contradictory answers he encountered on his spiritual trip. Most people relate to this. Harry's solution was to buy a sensory deprivation tank and shut out the world until he could observe his own mind and figure out how it worked. Then I describe the tank and get the person imagining what it would be like to be in one.

It took six weeks for the answers to unravel for Harry, but when they did, he realized that there was a much quicker way for a person to unravel his or her own answers. That is the beginning of Avatar.

Then I say, "You'll like this. " And I sit them down with a copy of *Living Deliberately* and have them read Chapter Six, "The Rapture."

When they finish I ask, "Are you interested in reading the rest of the book?" They usually say yes and I ask, "Okay, how would you like to pay for it?" and/or "Do I make out the receipt to you or your business?"

Creating an EPC* (from the Masters' Network Newsletter)

*EPC: Enlightened Planetary Civilization

Book sales are the key to creating Avatar students. FACT: If you were to prioritize everything you, as a Master, do in order of relative importance, book sales would be number one on the list.

Book sales are the key to creating Avatar students. FACT: Over 90 percent of the students who sign up for the Avatar Course have read at least one of the following: *Living Deliberately* or *ReSurfacing*. If you're talking to someone who hasn't read one of these books about anything other than buying and reading one of these books, you're wasting your time.

Book sales are the key to creating Avatar students. FACT: The all-time most successful Masters are those Masters who have sold the most books and have inserted a self-addressed post card for more information in every book.

Book sales are the key to creating Avatar students. FACT: Between 15 and 20 percent of the people who have bought and read one of these books have gone on to do Avatar.

Earlier this year, Star's Edge added the line *"Available from your local Avatar Master"* to all of its book advertising. The reason for this change in strategy is to create a faster and stronger connection between the book buyer and the Avatar Master.

When you sell a book, include a self-addressed post card for more information, or at the very least, place a sticker with your name and address inside the back cover. Whenever possible, get the name and address of the person buying the book, add them to your prospect list, and send them a Journal (or have Star's Edge send them a Journal).

TIP: You will find that you will have very little difficulty filling a *ReSurfacing* event, a Thoughtstorm, or a free lecture when you invite people who have already read a book. Book buyers are ready to become involved!

The simple action of selling one book a week could easily result in seven to ten new students a year. Think what would happen if you sold five books a week!

MAJOR POINT: <u>Book sales are the key to creating Avatar students.</u>

Book Marketing Tips

1. Get to know your customer. (Hint: they're the people who are most like you.) What are their needs and values? How will reading *Living Deliberately* or *ReSurfacing* benefit them? Your customer is in the unenviable position of not owning a copy of LD or ReS. Perceived benefits help him or her overcome the inertia of not owning LD or ReS.

2. Remind people that if they buy the book today, they will have the book available when they are ready to read it. (When the student is ready, the Master appears.)

3. Send a news release to your local media announcing that you are bringing Avatar to the area. Include your background and where you did the Master Course. Mention *Living Deliberately* and *ReSurfacing* and how you can be reached.

4. Who does book reviews in your local paper? Mention that *Living Deliberately* has sold over 200,000 copies and is currently available in 15 languages.

5. Check your local Chamber of Commerce, the Yellow Pages, and local newspaper for organizations in your area that might be hungry for a new speaker. It may take you several telephone calls to track down and talk to the person who schedules speakers. Tailor your

proposed talk to the group's interest (e.g., The Influence of Belief on _____) and offer some of the money from every book you sell after the talk to the group's membership fund. If the group publishes a newsletter, see if you can advertise a book and donate them a percentage of the profits.

6. Newsletters. Nearly everybody has a newsletter. Check with local printers and graphic arts departments to develop a list of newsletters in your area. Research advertising in the newsletter, who reads it, etc. Will they run book reviews or carry ads for a percentage of sales? Will they announce events?

If you are familiar with computer desktop publishing, offer to put together a newsletter for a group in exchange for your book ad in the newsletter.

7. Fax machines. Boy are there a lot of these! Consider a faxed book ad. New software and fax directories can really automate this process. It works while you sleep.

8. Are you a Professional Course graduate? Is there a grassroots local TV interview program? Most stations have them. Get a sense of the kind of story they are after—local event, expert, commentary—and offer your services. Finding the right person in a cooperative mood is crucial here. Supply them with books and Journals. Invite them to do *ReSurfacing* for free. Enlist their help in creating an enlightened planetary civilization.

9. Mom and Pop stores. Will they take five or ten books on consignment? What if you run a book ad and say available at _____?

10. Church bulletins. Many churches promote fellowship groups with discussions ranging from "How To Talk About Sex" to "What Is Faith?" Maybe it's time you went to church.

11. Hospitals. Hospital bookstores and book carts often include inspirational materials. Some waiting rooms have shelves of donated books. Well, what are you waiting for? While you are there, leave a complimentary copy at the-nurse's station.

12. Swap sheets and Penny-Savers. Here is a good place to test small ads. And the editors are hungry for interesting articles. Do they know there is an Avatar Master in town?

13. Book fairs, art fairs, festivals, trade shows, malls, and flea markets. A book table piled high with stock pulls lots of customers. Pass out redeemable $ off coupons or Avatar Bucks at the door to pull people to your table. At flea markets, turn other vendors into your book outlets by trading them five copies for something you want. An oversized book is good for attracting attention.

14. Libraries and colleges (college libraries). Is there a philosophy professor or psychology professor who will recommend *ReSurfacing* for his or her class? Sometimes it helps to remind them that they have an obligation to expose their students to current mental technologies.

15. Booksellers are great people. If they are not stocking Avatar books, order a few.

16. Will your local library accept copies of LD and ReS? A telephone call will tell. And write a press release letting the local media know that the books have been donated as a contribution to an enlightened planetary civilization.

17. Are there non-profit organizations (or public TV) soliciting donations in your community? Maybe they would buy discounted copies of *Living Deliberately* or *ReSurfacing* to

offer as gift incentives to their donors. And your name is in every copy! Could you use a tax deductible donation? Contact the right person and create a 30-minute program of your best interview clips and the Avatar video, "Take Back Your Life." Anyone who calls to make a pledge during your program receives *Living Deliberately* as a gift.

18. Make a list of all the benefits you can think of that a person would get from reading LD or ReS. Ask yourself, where are people currently seeking these benefits? Go to that place and hand out book flyers.

19. Submit Harry's *Avatar Journal* articles to your local newspapers and magazines for reprint. Editors of newsletters are always looking for good copy. Be sure to add your name and contact information so they can order the books from you.

20. Offer a schedule of free attention demonstrations at your local bookstores, health food stores, and New Age shops. Provide them with handouts and posters showing the times you will be available. Let the bookstore, etc. stock and sell the books. (*ReSurfacing* exercises 6-9)

Bonus Tips

21. Bulletin boards. Use a poster with tear-off order forms. Laundromat bulletin boards are tops, followed by beauty salons and waiting rooms.

22. Who will package one of your book flyers with every order?

23. Bumper sticker. READ LIVING DELIBERATELY.

24. Include a book flyer in every letter you write and every bill you pay.

25. How much would a billboard for *Living Deliberately* and *ReSurfacing* cost? Who might contribute to defray the cost?

26. *Living Deliberately* book tee-shirts? Why not?

27. Ever hear of Toastmasters? Try your local telephone book.

28. Ask your mother who she knows who would be interested in a *Living Deliberately* book.

29. Add a book ad to the back of your business card.

30. Gyms have classes; why not lectures? Exercise your mental muscles.

31. Answering machine sales. "Hi, I can't come to the phone right now, but if you're calling to place an order for the *Living Deliberately* book, please leave a message."

32. Advertise *Living Deliberately* in this theater. Available at the following locations: (how much will the local bookstore contribute toward your ad?)

Outrageous Tips

33. Paint a *Living Deliberately* ad on the side of your car or van.

34. Mount a *Living Deliberately* billboard on the top of your car.

35. Load a *Living Deliberately* billboard in the back of your pickup.

36. Park your vehicle by the entrance of a major sporting event, concert, theme park, etc., for a million dollars worth of free advertising.

37. Build a *Living Deliberately* book that someone can wear.

38. Build a 4 x 7 foot *Living Deliberately* book to take to your talks and events.

39. Paint a *Living Deliberately* book on the side of a building (with permission).

40. Wear a hat that looks like a *Living Deliberately* book.

41. Thoughtstorming with other Masters will turn up more tips.

Major Point

Book sales are the key to creating Avatar students.

Chapter 10

Inspire and Involve

Resource	Effort	Sub-Product
5. A person who owns an Avatar book, tape or tape set.	Inspire and involve. Has the material been read? What did they think? Encourage them to apply the ideas in their own thinking.	A person who would like to experience an Avatar process (a friend of Avatar).

inspire 1. *to instruct or infuse with spiritual knowledge* 2. *to stimulate or impel to some creative effort*

Immediate telephone follow-up on book buyers is overkill. It is more likely to be perceived as annoying than as helpful or informative. Before you call them, you should get them to originate to you that they have some interest in Avatar. How?

Letters, faxes and e-mail. Written communications are generally more welcomed and are given more attention than unsolicited telephone calls.

Writing has the added advantage of allowing you to compose your thoughts and to deliberately choose how and what you say. In the long run, it is also less time consuming, because you can use the same letter for multiple customers.

Follow-up Letters

Before you start composing the contents of your letters, give some thought to organizing your correspondence and improving its general appearance. If you don't have a computer with word-processing software, now is the time to get one. (If you don't know how to use a computer, see Chapter 4.)

Once you are comfortably familiar with computers, take the next step and learn how to set up a database. A database is a computer program that stores information in records composed of adjustable-size, fill-in-the-blank spaces called fields. You set up the database by defining the fields of information you want. Field examples are: date, first name, last name, address, city, state, zip or postal code, country, level of resource, sortcode, notes. Each record in the database contains these fields of data on a single item. In this case, the item is your potential Avatar student.

Now here's how it works. Each time you select **add a record**, you get a blank form with each of the fields ready to be filled in. You type in the first name, move to the next field, type in the last name, move to the next field, etc. When you get to the field that you named **sortcode**, you type in a code that you create, e.g., BB for book buyer, CC for contact and connection, RS for ReSurfer, HP for hot prospect and so on. You can call up a record at any time and change the data in any field.

Now, you want to send a letter to all your book buyers to inspire and involve them. You go into your word processing program and you compose a letter. (Suggestion: Use a serif font as it market tests better than sans-serif fonts.) Suppose you compose a debriefing letter on what happened at the last Saturday night Thoughtstorm—describe what Thoughtstorming is, describe where it was, who was there, how long it lasted, what questions were Thoughtstormed. A nice touch is have your prospects send you their opinions on the question in exchange for your sending them the corecept arrived at by the group.

Your word processing software has a feature called merge. Merge is a technique of adding personal information stored in a database to a form letter that you create in the word-processing software. You tell the computer to print a copy of the letter and insert (merge) the name and address of every sortcode = BB in the database.

Do you want address labels? No problem. Your word processor can merge and print them on peel-off labels. Print an extra set and send them to Star's Edge for a Journal mailing.

Isn't technology wonderful?

But wait a minute, this looks just like another form letter. You need to make it more distinctive. How about a little handwritten message or question on each letter? For example, "We missed you Friday. Hope you can make it next week. Do you have any input on our Thoughtstorm question?" or "Did you get the calendar of events that I mailed to you?" or "Why don't you call me and let me know about your progress with the book? I'd like to know what you thought.," or "Do you have an e-mail address or a fax machine?"

What goes with the letter? How about an interesting photo from your last event? Photos are inexpensive to reproduce, and you can write a message on the back of a photo. "That's me on the right with Laura, our newest Avatar." Write on your envelope, "Please handle with care, photo enclosed."

What else can you send? How about a *ReSurfacing* book flyer, a copy of a success article from *Messages from the Heart* or a success story from one of your own students and/or an RSVP form for your next event? How about a return postcard that they can use to send you the names and addresses of friends they would like to receive a complimentary copy of the *Avatar Journal*? How about an AVATAR frequently asked questions page? How about the agenda of your next *ReSurfacing* workshop or Avatar Course? How about a three-month event calendar? How about creating a group newsletter? How about a Perspective article? How about a rental agreement for one of your copies of the "Take Back Your Life" video or the *ReSurfacing* audio workshop tapes? How about a consciousness opinion poll? How about your e-mail address and an invitation to visit the *starsedge.com* web page? How about a request for anecdotes about unusual consciousness phenomena? How about an unused postage stamp? Or an invitation to participate in a well-publicized community project that your group is doing? What else?

Whoa, you're going to need a bigger envelope! Just kidding. You don't sent it all at once; you send something every week.

Involvement

It is important to remember that involvement begins as a spectator sport. Participatory involvement comes later. You involve a person's attention first. They don't have to show up at one of your events to become involved. They only have to hear about what happened to start becoming involved. Who's going to tell them? You are. You involve them with easily understandable, fascinating and valuable information and anecdotes.

You involve them in the part of your life that has to do with Avatar. You involve them with the ideas and the language of Avatar. You involve them with appreciation and compassion in the connect-up process of creating an enlightened planetary civilization. You become a rational, helpful voice in their world. The goal is to **make Avatar real for them.** Don't get sidetracked into promoting the wonderful-world-of-me or your cosmetic business or the details of your daughter's birthday party. That's personal, as in personality, identity, approval. What you want to create is an inviting reality. Realities involve people; personalities compete with people.

You let them see your dedication. You tell them you are delivering Avatar to help people be happier, live a better life, be more successful. You prove it to them with student testimonials and life-changing realizations. You communicate the same message in different ways until they realize that you could be doing the same thing for them.

Telephone Calls

After a person has responded to one of your mailings (or has received numerous mailings without responding), a telephone call is in order. Avoid times when the person is likely to be busy or tired. The best telephone windows are between 10 AM and noon, 2 PM and 4 PM on the weekends. You should set these times aside as your call periods. Make a little contest with yourself to see how many calls you can complete on a weekend.

Before you telephone, it's a good idea to have an outline of the information you want to find out and the information you want to convey. You're going to keep some general notes on what the person says, so have some paper handy. If the person is busy, find out when is a good time to arrange a chat.

Have they done Avatar yet? No? Oh, good, that's one of the things you wanted to talk to them about. Have you done any meditation? Chat. Chat. Chat. Do they know there is an event this weekend?

Chat. Chat. Chat. Bring a friend. Lovely to talk with you. Bye.

If they don't come, don't worry. Just make sure they get a fascinating briefing on what happened at the event, and who had wins, and what they missed. They'll come next time.

Chapter 11

Events

Resource	Effort	Sub-Product
6. Avatar prospect	Get them to an experiential Avatar event that stimulates realizations about life. Describe the expected results of Avatar.	A person who has tested some elementary Avatar techniques with good results and has moved doing Avatar to the top of his or her priority list.

An event is for people who know something about Avatar. It has the goal of generating experiences and realizations (through participatory involvement) that lead a person to register for the full Avatar Course. Its sub-product is a person who is excited about doing Avatar and has moved it to the top of his or her priority list.

Events are specialized mini-workshops using processes from *ReSurfacing*.

The first step of an event, which is done before the event is announced, is the planning and organizing of an Avatar delivery. (See Effort #7, Chapter 6, "Productive Efforts"). This includes spaces for study and exercise, travel directions, housing requirements, availability of meals, course schedule plus any extras that add value to the course. This is often a cooperative creation with other Masters. All of this information should be brought together in an attractive promotion package that includes preregistration forms.

Now you are ready to plan and stage an event. (Always have a plan for an event.)

Events are primarily for book buyers who have already been interested and involved through journals, mailings, and personal contact. Everyone present has at least fantasized about doing Avatar. The usual event fee is kept low (US$25-US$50) and includes a copy of the *ReSurfacing* book. Participants are encouraged to prepay and preregister or at least make a commitment to attend. Accompanying friends are welcomed.

The event can be broadly announced and welcomes everyone, but the target audience is level 5 and level 6 resources (Reference Chapter 6, "Productive Efforts"). In addition to the book table in the room, there is now a registration table.

Events are longer and more experiential than presentations.

Plan For a Typical Event

1. Everyone present has a *ReSurfacing* workbook.

2. Acknowledgment and expectation worm: *"Thank you for coming. Today will be full of lessons, surprises, and realizations. You are going to discover that a lot more is happening than what is visible."*

3. Announce a goal for the event: *"By the end of this event, everyone here is going to have at least one good reason for doing the full Avatar Course."*

4. Quiet the space with introductions and expressions of gratitude: *"Since we are going to be working together, we are all going to have to share the awkwardness of introductions. So each of you, please stand up, say your name and something you'd like the group to know about you, and finally tell the group one thing that you are really grateful for today. "*

These steps should be written where everyone can see them.

"I will start. My name is _____ _____ and I am _____(e.g., an amateur computer enthusiast) and I am grateful for _____." (e.g., being able to control my own time).

Don't avoid this step, because it begins the integration process from individual into group. Any embarrassment that appears is only egocentrism dissolving.

5. Discovery of will: *"What do you think is the most important quality a person can possess?"* Take as many answers as people want to give. Usual answers are kindness, love, freedom. *"What determines if you're kind or loving or ____? Is it just a matter of luck?"* (Let people participate with answers if they wish, but you control the questions.) *"Have you ever failed to be an example of this quality, even though you think it is important? What happened? Something just took over, right?"*

Continue this discussion until everyone realizes that they don't always act deliberately. Introduce the idea of will. Have the group open to page 25 of *ReSurfacing* and take turns each reading a paragraph aloud. Also have the definitions read.

6. Introduce Exercise 2 and send the group out for a fifteen-minute walk to notice things and decide how they would describe them.

7. *"How did you do? Anyone notice anything happening to their perception?"*

8. Do Exercise 5 with the group.

Afterwards, *"How did you do? Anyone notice anything happening to their mind?"*

9. Have the group take turns reading aloud page 33, "Attention."

10. Do Exercise 6 with the group.

11. Have the group take turns reading aloud page 37, "Contemplations and Discussions."

12. Discuss page 37, Question 1. End with *"Instead of trying to describe where attention comes from, try to feel it."* Pause and then go right into the Expansion Exercise (P. 90.) After this exercise, tell everyone to take a fifteen-minute break to enjoy and integrate.

13. **Commercial:** Return from break. Pass out your promotion package* and tell everybody about the next Avatar delivery. Go over Sections 1-3 of the Avatar Materials page in the back of *ReSurfacing.* Answer questions. Read the list of some of the expected results.

* See page 76.

- Learn how to manage your beliefs.
- Learn how to take control of your life.
- Learn to better understand yourself.
- Learn to free yourself of self-sabotaging behaviors.
- Learn to see others as they truly are.
- Learn to achieve a meditative mind state and peak experiences at will.
- Learn to stay calm even while others are losing their cool.
- Learn how to magnetize your mind to attract what you desire.
- Learn how to recognize and resolve self-doubts.

- Learn how to pull your own strings and run your own life.

- Learn to live deliberately, proudly, and boldly.

Ask, *"Has anyone found at least one good reason for doing Avatar yet?"*

14. Continue with the group's reading aloud pages 45-46, "Freeing Attention and Insight."

15. Help the group through Exercise 10 (p. 47) and end with a discussion of Question 13 (p. 48).

16. Option: Have the group pair up and show them how to run Exercise 12, "Releasing Fixed Attention."

17. Option: Have the group read and complete the exercises in the Belief Section. (pp. 75-83.)

18. Have them think of a person they like. You read the steps aloud and have them do the Compassion Exercise on that person. (p. 67). Repeat the exercise on a person they don't like. *"How did you do? Anyone notice anything happening to their awareness?"*

19. Hand out debrief forms to be filled out and collected. Announce that anyone who found at least one good reason to do Avatar should talk with you (or another Master) at the registration table. Before they leave, invite them to read pages 110 to 114.

Use what works best for you from the above, and feel free (after you gain some experience) to modify anything that results in more enrollments for your Avatar delivery.

Chapter 12

Avatar Students

Resource	Effort	Sub-Product
7. Pre-Avatar student	Present the agenda for the course. Assist them to register and arrive.	An Avatar student

Always ask a step 6 sub-product (a step 7 resource),"Are you ready to sign up for Avatar or do you need to think about it some more?"

If they're ready, sign them up and don't waste your time selling. If they need to think about it some more, start selling.

Selling Avatar

The fact that a Master sometimes has to sell someone into doing Avatar is another confirmation of the strangeness of the current civilizations on this planet. There is a barrier of skepticism and suspicion that you must navigate successfully to create an enlightened planetary civilization. It is a culturally inherited labyrinth of irrationality that stands between some individuals and the enlightenment offered by Avatar.

Eventually the principles of Avatar will work their way into society and be regarded as essential social skills. But until that occurs, you are faced with transforming civilizations one customer at a time.

A prospective student should be regarded as a customer and be treated with the same sales assistance that any successful enterprise uses to create new customers. The difference is that your customers are not going to end up feeling they were sold; they're going to end up feeling they were saved.

You are lucky that your product is Avatar. It has such broad applications that you can offer satisfying benefits tailored to fit a person's needs. Just remember that you have to deliver on your promises, so don't create expectations the customer can't achieve. Offer the tools. Never deceive a customer. Just present honestly how the Avatar tools have been used by others.

Things learned on the course:

- Learn how to manage your beliefs.
- Learn how to take control of your life.
- Learn to better understand yourself.
- Learn to free yourself of self-sabotaging behaviors.
- Learn to see others as they truly are.
- Learn to achieve a meditative mind state and peak experiences at will.
- Learn to stay calm even while others are losing their cool.
- Learn how to magnetize your mind to attract what you desire.
- Learn how to recognize and resolve self-doubts.
- Learn how to pull your own strings and run your own life.
- Learn to live deliberately, proudly, and boldly.

When a person understands that learning and using the Avatar tools is a rational action leading to personal (as well as social) benefits, the sale is half closed. The final step is to create a mental scenario of the course in which a person can see himself or herself doing Avatar.*

Features and benefits that you might use to help the student create a mental scenario of the course:

* This is where your effort #7 will pay off.

- It is easy to learn.
- It is effective.
- It is broadly available and respected.
- It is not confrontational or embarrassing.
- You're not lost in a group.
- The materials are well organized and presented in a logical sequence.
- There is a personal trust between you and the Avatar Master.
- There are no doctrines or beliefs you have to subscribe to.
- The course is self-paced and empowers you as source.
- The course recognizes your own unique beingness.
- You'll discover that there is nothing that rivals Avatar in the fill-in-missing-pieces department.
- You reconnect with your own intuitive guidance.
- You become part of a global network of mutually empowering individuals.
- If you like, you can review the course in exotic locations. (Courses have been given in Nepal, on the Nile, along the Amazon, in the Great Pyramid, in an Andes monastery, on board a Pacific freighter, in the Australian outback, in the Icelandic hot springs region.)

You treat the student's vision of being on the course like a primary. The only things left to handle are the secondaries.

Sometimes a person's rational response is submerged by secondary concerns. What will others think? Shouldn't the money be used for something else? Am I being selfish? Maybe I can get it cheaper. What if it doesn't work?

You can handle each of these secondary concerns by listening to the person (that's the exaggeration part) and then reminding the person that doing Avatar is the best long-range solution to the concern. "They'll probably discover that some of their fellow students had the same concerns (that's the ...*and now the primary* part)."

The customer says, "I can't afford it." You listen.

You say, "How much are your self-limiting beliefs costing you every day? It is not unusual for a student to discover that his or her unrealized potential is a hundred times more expensive than the investment in Avatar. Doesn't it make sense to improve the rest of your life for a few pennies a day?"

Or the customer says, "Yeah, someday." You listen.

You say, "Let's plan backwards from your sitting in a classroom and learning to use the Avatar tools until we reach a doable step."

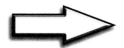 (Self-imposed limitations and ignorance of the product are the only things that keep a person from doing Avatar.)

The Buying Decision

The prospective customer of Avatar reaches his or her buying decision through a combination of intuitional, rational, and emotional processes. Each of these processes can be addressed and accelerated by a skillful Master. The intuitional process is accelerated by the Master's primaries, the rational process is accelerated by information on the world mission of Avatar and the successes of previous students, and the emotional process is accelerated by reminding the prospect of relevant benefits.

Relevancy

Relevant information is data that offers a possible solution to the obstacle or problem that one has attention on. For example, the combination to a safe is relevant information to someone who wants to open the safe, but probably irrelevant to someone who is fixing a sink.

In order to convey relevant information to some people, you may have to free some of their attention from the obstacle. You free enough attention so that they can recognize the possibility that you are offering them relevant information.

"Hey you," you shout. "Hey, hey you, do you want to open that safe? 17-13-45!" This gets their attention. "Here is the combination. 17-13-45."

That's typically how you provide relevant information to someone with attention fixed on a physical obstacle. (Of course, if you give them a wrong combination, it's going to be tougher to get their attention again.)

It's not quite as easy to provide relevant information to someone whose attention is stuck on a mental obstacle. You can't just shout, "Discreate it." That doesn't work. That's like finding someone pushing on a door and offering the advice, "Push." It just fixes their attention more.

The principle is this: you have to free up enough of their attention so they recognize that you are offering them relevant information. And then you'd better be sure your information is relevant.

More on the Intuitional Decision Process

Intuition is a higher order of instinct. Another way of saying this is that the quality we call instinct in animal consciousness is called intuition in higher consciousness.

At both levels, the essence of the internal message is, "This is the right (or wrong) thing to do." And at both levels, the apparent source of this message is beyond the individual's ordinary waking consciousness.

Many exploitive businesses (health threatening, environmentally threatening, nonessential consumables, etc.) have to sell over a person's sense of, "This is the right thing to do." These businesses do not consider intuition beneficial to the selling process, hence they try to disconnect people from this inner direction with cleverly phrased repeating mental circuits that drown out the more subtle intuitive guidance. *"Winston tastes good like a cigarette should."*

Not Avatar

When you find out what people value as important and then show them that **NOT** doing Avatar, **NOT** developing their potential, is a transgression against this value, you will awaken their intuitive processes.

You reconnect the prospect with his own intuitive process. "Avatar is the right thing to do. Managing your own beliefs is a right thing to do. Learning more about yourself is a right thing to do. Exploring consciousness, creating relationships, coaxing people toward peace and tolerance are all right things to do. Creating an enlightened planetary civilization is a right thing to do."

This isn't done as an advertising jingle. It's offering the person a thread to follow back to his or her own intuitive process. It is probably the most powerful marketing tool ever conceived, but it won't sell a destructive product. Fortunately, it is not very useful for any product other than enlightenment.

The Ethics of Persuasion

Persuasion can be more compassionate than truth. Communicating truth is giving someone the facts and letting them look out for themselves. Persuasion is extended responsibility. Faced with a choice, a person may not have the experience to make anything more than a guess. Their ability to calculate future probability is very low. On the other hand, your experience with the outcome of various decisions can make your persuasion not only ethical, but can morally obligate you to offer advice and direction.

Things that can persuade a change of mind:
1. Recognizing a personal benefit
2. Potential to discover new information
3. Exciting future goals (unpleasant future consequence)
4. Intuitive hunch
5. Emotional involvement

Time

Coming to a positive decision may take a matter of minutes or it may extend over a long period of time. A significant number of potential students, perhaps as high as 25 percent, circle the fringe of Avatar, reading the Journal, talking to Masters or other Avatars for a year or more before they finally make the commitment to do Avatar.

Master Anecdote on Incentive

One Avatar Master we know worked on her husband to do Avatar for eight years. He was intuitively and rationally attracted to Avatar and thought it was a nice thing **for her**. But for himself, he didn't believe the personal benefits from doing it outweighed the inconveniences. "Someday, maybe," was the only commitment he'd make.

One day he and his wife shared a disturbing experience. Their house was broken into and robbed. She took it as a world lesson, discreated her resistance to the event, and refocused on creating a preferred reality. But he was angry. The anger crippled him. He couldn't work. He couldn't sleep. He couldn't direct his anger at the thief, because the thief was gone. So he directed it at her.

Finally, she told him to handle his anger. What an idea! The desire incentive suddenly appeared.

He did Avatar with another Master. At first he was hopeless, and there was no way he could change a viewpoint that the world had created. The Master ignored his asserted limitations and was routinely, ruthlessly insistent upon, "Now the primary."

Of course, his breakthrough came, and it changed his life. He loved Avatar and is now a happy, still-married, Star Master!

The Continuous Course
(from a talk by Harry)

Avra and I went to California in 1988 to deliver Avatar to eleven students. The plan was to complete the delivery and come home, but a remarkable thing happened. Somewhere around day four of the delivery, our new Avatars started calling their friends. I was recruited to give nightly talks for the friends. Most of the new Avatars had completed their initiation session, and they were glowing. Their friends wanted to sign up. So we continued the course. We flew in another woman from our office in New York to handle contact and registration. She got Avatars to introduce her to more friends, and she began a big call-in. We finally had to close registration so we could finish and leave. In the end we were there for six weeks and delivered to seventy-five people. The point: there is a natural momentum of excitement that builds up around an Avatar delivery. Masters should use that excitement and keep a delivery running for as long as anyone signs up.

Index

A

destroy, 103
destructive, 50, 141
dictate, 22, 57
dictatorial, 22
die, 7
difficult, 26-27, 38, 82, 84
difficulties, 1, 56
difficulty, 66, 88, 92, 112-113, 115
dilettantes, 43
diligence, 74
disagreement, 27
disappear, 57
disappoint, 85, 91
discernment, 50, 55, 89, 112
discipline, 41
discouraged, 5, 8
discouragement, 5, 8, 37-38, 44-45, 75
discreate, 4, 16, 26, 59, 140
discreated, 14, 20, 142
discretion, 55
disease, 9
dishonesty, 6
disincarnate, 21-22
disposition, 55
disseminate, 45, 47-48, 53
distress, 55
disturbing, 142
divine, 15
diving, 27
doctrines, 137
doingness, 37
doubt, 6
dreams, 4-5, 9, 49, 68, 72-73, 93, 106-107

E

edge, 8, 29, 54, 70, 85, 109, 115, 125
Edison, 42
effective, 101, 137
efficiency, 45, 49
efficient, 50, 74
ego, 18-19, 22, 27-28, 110, 131
embarrassment, 88, 108, 131, 137
emergency, 108-109
emotion, 9, 13-14, 68, 91, 139, 141
empower, 39, 48-51, 71, 75, 137
encourage, 5, 65-66, 84, 88, 123, 130
endeavor, 10
endure, 41
enemies, 49, 79

F

loving, 17, 131
luck, 44, 46, 131
lucky, 17, 136

M

machine, 117, 120, 125
magic, 25, 30, 46, 103
manual, 42
meditate, 101
meditation, 90, 127, 132
memory, 6, 17
men, 99
merge, 124-125
minds, 20, 88
miracle, 18, 25
misaligned, 55
misalignment, 6, 55
mistake, 16
mistakes, 21, 37, 55, 105, 111
model, 53-54, 74
modeling, 19
modest, 54
monastery, 137
monologues, 17
monopolize, 90
motion, 15, 20
motivate, 9-10, 14, 41, 57, 59, 73
motives, 55, 58, 109
mystical, 69

N

nature, 15, 32, 74
navigate, 135
negative, 72
neglect, 59
negotiation, 77
no-brainer, 27

O

objection, 33, 113
objective, 15, 105
observe, 15, 17, 21, 27-28, 56-57, 59, 86, 89, 106, 112, 114
obstacle, 112-113, 139-140
obstruction, 38-39, 42, 107, 113
opinion, 10, 55, 110, 124, 126
opportunities, 51, 88
organization, 40, 49-50, 116, 118

organize, 39, 49, 78
organizing, 76, 123, 129
outflow, 81, 87
overwhelm, 35, 63, 82, 86

P

pain, 88
painful, 41, 88
panic, 41
paths, 29, 37, 58
patience, 59
patterns, 15, 26, 106
peace, 58, 141
peaceful, 68
peak, 76, 132, 136
perceive, 14, 16, 18, 44, 69, 87, 116, 123
perception, 25
perceptive, 55
performance, 37-40, 45, 48-50, 59, 66
perseverance, 27
persistence, 26, 66
personality, 69, 110, 127
perspective, 15, 126
persuasion, 5, 21, 94, 100, 141
pledge, 57, 118
power, 10, 17, 25-26, 31-35, 40, 49, 55, 59, 92, 100, 102-103, 113, 141
predict, 14-15, 18, 41
prejudice, 82
presence, 14, 81, 88, 108
presentations, 69, 93-97, 99, 101, 103, 105, 107, 109, 130
press, 66, 101, 110, 118
pressure, 25, 27, 30, 49, 109
pretend, 100
pretending, 75
pretense, 14, 20, 55, 113
problem, 13, 91-92, 106, 124-125, 139
project, 5, 17, 40-41, 126
projected, 14, 41
projections, 18
promise, 84
promises, 136
propaganda, 110
prospects, 42, 65, 79
psyche, 82
psychic, 22
psychologist, 94

psychology, 118
purposes, 68, 77

R

rapport, 14
rapture, 114
reaction, 17, 21, 86
reactivated, 26
reactivates, 26
reactively, 103
realities, 27, 127
realization, 44, 46, 58, 65, 75, 78, 127, 129-130
realize, 17, 47, 67-68, 75, 86, 111, 127
reasonable, 3-5, 9
receptivity, 25
recognition, 13, 54, 56
recovery, 21
referral, 82, 84-85
refunds, 95
regret, 56, 88
rejection, 54, 88
rekindle, 93
relationship, 9, 13, 16-18, 26, 41, 67, 72-73, 84, 108-109, 141
relative, 114
reliable, 39
relief, 101
religion, 21
reluctance, 90
rely, 30, 73, 99
remarkable, 143
reminiscing, 85
repent, 57
repentance, 57
reporter, 108-110
reports, 109
representative, 53
reputation, 6-7
resentment, 59
resist, 14, 16, 18, 21, 41, 56, 112, 142
resonated, 44
respect, 13-15, 56, 58, 72, 82, 137
response, 110, 138
responsible, 22-23, 31, 39, 48, 76, 92, 141
right-to-influence, 32
risk, 50, 109
rituals, 82
routine, 39, 45, 47-48
rumor, 108

S

T

touch, 124
touching, 74
transform, 66
transformation, 55
transforming, 135
trap, 14-15
trapped, 29, 68
trouble, 16, 54, 73, 86, 88
trust, 20, 137
truths, 20

U

unaligned, 50
uncertainty, 38
undertake, 11, 18, 38, 41
unexplored, 56
ungrounded, 16
unhappy, 7, 16
unique, 137
unity, 6
unknowns, 14, 75
unpleasant, 141
unpopular, 22, 50
unpredictable, 18
unproductive, 39, 48-49
unrewarded, 66
unseen, 130

V

validation, 55, 87
valuable, 15, 59-60, 74, 84-85, 126
variables, 108
vicarious, 73
victim, 17, 20, 59, 110
viewpoints, 13-14, 87
views, 3
violation, 34
violence, 17
visible, 55, 58, 130
vision, 40, 49-50, 138
visionary, 5
vulnerability, 75, 106
vulnerable, 92

sincere, 55, 58-60, 67, 79, 87, 112
skepticism, 135
space, 15-16, 20, 53, 99, 130
spectator, 126
spirit, 22, 99
spiritual, 22, 41, 68-69, 77, 89-90, 114, 123
spokesperson, 108-109
Star's Edge, 126
steal, 6
stealing, 7
stonecutter, 7
strangeness, 135
stranger, 21, 43
strangers, 45
strategy, 115
strawberries, 73
strength, 69
strengthening, 19
stress, 69
stressed, 59
stubborn, 26, 58
stubbornness, 13
study, 27-28, 38, 42, 69, 78, 96, 129
sub-product, 39, 48-49, 64-67, 70, 72, 76, 81, 93, 111,
    123, 129, 135
substance, 15, 20, 56
subtle, 140
succumb, 63
succumbed, 44
susceptible, 30
suspicion, 82, 87, 135
sympathy, 55
systematized, 49

T

talks, 69, 93, 103, 120, 143
team, 49
teammates, 39, 48
teams, 49
tendency, 15-16, 19-20, 45
terminal, 27, 81
terrain, 13
testimonials, 65, 81, 127
therapy, 19
thoughtstorm, 77, 83, 115, 121, 124-125
threaten, 56
threatening, 82, 108, 140
Toastmasters, 120
tolerance, 10, 141

touch, 124
touching, 74
transform, 66
transformation, 55
transforming, 135
trap, 14-15
trapped, 29, 68
trouble, 16, 54, 73, 86, 88
trust, 20, 137
truths, 20

U

unaligned, 50
uncertainty, 38
undertake, 11, 18, 38, 41
unexplored, 56
ungrounded, 16
unhappy, 7, 16
unique, 137
unity, 6
unknowns, 14, 75
unpleasant, 141
unpopular, 22, 50
unpredictable, 18
unproductive, 39, 48-49
unrewarded, 66
unseen, 130

V

validation, 55, 87
valuable, 15, 59-60, 74, 84-85, 126
variables, 108
vicarious, 73
victim, 17, 20, 59, 110
viewpoints, 13-14, 87
views, 3
violation, 34
violence, 17
visible, 55, 58, 130
vision, 40, 49-50, 138
visionary, 5
vulnerability, 75, 106
vulnerable, 92

W

Y

Z

Avatar®: The Advanced Courses

Section IVA of the
Avatar Materials

The Master Course

**An expedition
into the deeper regions
of Avatar.**

- What sticks a person into a viewpoint or creation?

- What are the mechanics behind the Avatar initiation?

- How can you change an entire structure of beliefs in a few minutes?

Nine days

    For times and locations contact the Advance Scheduling Registrar at Star's Edge International.

407-788-3090 *tel.*
407-788-1052 *fax*
avatar@avatarhq.com *e-mail*

Section IVB of the
Avatar Materials

The Professional Course

Discover the amazement of being.

- What is the relationship between stress, awareness and being?

- What makes a person unable to change?

- What are the components of life?

Seven days

For times and locations contact the Advance Scheduling Registrar at Star's Edge International.

407-788-3090 *tel.*
407-788-1052 *fax*
avatar@avatarhq.com *e-mail*

Section V of the
Avatar Materials

The Wizard Course

- What effort is behind the creation of mind?

- Can creative study accelerate your evolution?

- What is the danger of enlightenment?

Thirteen days

For times and locations contact the Advance Scheduling Registrar at Star's Edge International.

407-788-3090 *tel.*
407-788-1052 *fax*
avatar@avatarhq.com *e-mail*